What's a Smart Woman Like You Doing In a Place Like This?

What's a Smart Woman Like You Doing In a Place Like This?

HOMEMAKING ON PURPOSE

Mary Ann Froehlich

Wolgemuth & Hyatt, Publishers, Inc.
Brentwood, Tennessee

The mission of Wolgemuth & Hyatt, Publishers, Inc. is to publish and distribute books that lead individuals toward:

- A personal faith in the one true God: Father, Son, and Holy Spirit;

- A lifestyle of practical discipleship; and

- A worldview that is consistent with the historic, Christian faith.

Moreover, the Company endeavors to accomplish this mission at a reasonable profit and in a manner which glorifies God and serves His Kingdom.

© 1989 by Mary Ann Froehlich. All rights reserved
Published November 1989. First Edition
Printed in the United States of America
96 95 94 93 92 91 90   8 7 6 5 4 3 2 (Second printing June 1990)

Unless otherwise noted, all scripture quotations are from the Holy Bible, New International Version. © 1973, 1978, 1984 International Bible Society. Used by permission of Zondervan Bible Publishers.

Wolgemuth & Hyatt, Publishers, Inc.
1749 Mallory Lane, Suite 110, Brentwood, Tennessee 37027.
Printed in the United States of America.

Library of Congress Cataloging-in-Publication Data

Froehlich, Mary Ann, 1955–
    What's a smart woman like you doing in a place like this? :
homemaking on purpose / Mary Ann Froehlich. — 1st ed.
        p.   cm.
    Includes bibliographical references.
    ISBN 0-943497-77-9 : $9.95
    1. Housewives — United States. 2. Mothers — United States. 3. Self-
respect. I. Title.
HQ759.F745 1989
    640 — dc20   89-24929
                                                                      CIP

Dedicated to my husband, parents, and
Mary Pride, the most hardworking,
persevering guides I know

and to the professional, industrious
women of First Baptist Church, Benicia

CONTENTS

ACKNOWLEDGMENTS

T hank you to Virginia Hiramatsu for her excellent typing work and constant support.

Also I am deeply grateful to Mary Pride: "She was in a class by herself. It is not often that someone comes along who is a true friend and a good writer" (E.B. White, *Charlotte's Web*).

"For I know the plans that I have for you," declares the Lord, "plans for welfare and not for calamity to give you a future and a hope."

(Jeremiah 29:11, NASB)

ONE

PROFESSIONALS ON THE HOMEFRONT

Eight years ago my life radically changed. As with most of God's greatest gifts to us, this gift was tied with ribbons of tears and heartache. Happily immersed in a fast-moving lifestyle common to young couples starting out in a large metropolitan city, I was working as a therapist at a children's hospital in a job that I loved, attending graduate school in the evenings, teaching at a nearby college, and sharing the music ministry position with my husband in our church. In addition, we kept a busy social calendar and were working on projects in our first home. The only reason that our marriage survived was that my husband and I, being good friends, did many of these activities together, and his intense schedule made mine look like I was standing still! Neither one of us was ever at home waiting for the other and feeling neglected. We had committed to spend these years "getting established."

One day after work my husband announced that he was leaving on a business trip for the northern part of the state. He knew of an excellent job opportunity near there and wanted to interview as practice for upcoming interviews in our own area. We both laughed. We would *never* consider uprooting and moving, but the interview would be good experience.

A week later I sat in shock in our kitchen. John was telling me that the company had offered him the job on the spot. It was an excellent promotion filled with long-dreamed-of opportunities. We would be living in a small town away from a major city or university. He wanted to take the job! I was speechless. My mind was racing. Biblically, I knew that I was called to support my husband and follow him no matter the cost. I could trust that God knew what He was doing with my life.

Why Me?

But the sacrifice was overwhelming! *I* had never lived out of the area. *I* had a lifetime support system of family and friends. *I* was starting the last year of my doctoral program and was in the midst of my dissertation research in my hospital position. *I* was preparing for my doctoral recital. My job future was bright after degree completion. By God's grace, *I* was reaping the rewards of years of hard work. By God's grace, *I* was being required to sacrifice it all. My life was crumbling, and I entered a grieving process. Separation from family and friends, our church, and my work was a death. You have noticed that the operative word was *I*.

Yet, our God is a loving father and is very tender with His hurting children. Miraculously, funds were provided for me to fly back one day a week for a year to complete my doctoral work and see family and friends. God had prepared a new life for me, but He knew that I wouldn't survive the "cold turkey approach." He would ease the transition.

Slowly I became accustomed to small-town life. There were no job possibilities for me. I lived for that one day a week that I could return to my "other life." John was completely immersed in his new job which added to my loneliness. Again, God sent out a lifeline through a group of caring women from the church we were attending. They treated my open wounds with love and kindness and were very patient with my long adjustment. John and I had always been in the position of ministering to others. It was time for me to be still, focus completely on God, and *receive* ministry. My real education was just beginning.

Initially, I found that I had nothing in common with this group of women who stayed at home to care for their husbands and children. I enjoyed their company and admired them for their dedication, but their world was a foreign culture to me! Slowly I learned that each woman had her own unique specialization and that many of the women had college and graduate degrees. They had *chosen* to stay home and care for their families. On my weekly trip back to the city, less and less could I quietly tolerate the subtle undercurrent of comments referring to "housewives" made by my friends. I tried to remember if I had made those ignorant comments and shuddered.

"Dr. Mom"

Halfway through the year God sent the greatest gift of all. I became pregnant with a baby that John and I very much wanted. My life had finally slowed down to a point where we could consider starting our family. I realized that if we had remained in our previous lifestyle, "the right time for having a baby" would never have come. I was thrilled to be expecting our first child.

I had assumed that I would seek serious employment after adjusting to the area and completing my doctorate, but my pregnancy changed everything! For many reasons, I had always known that, if financially possible, I wanted to stay home to be a mother to my children. In addition to Biblical conviction, years spent working with children had shown me a clear difference between children who were the focus of full-time mothers and those who seemed to fall through the cracks of dual career schedules.

My main reason for wanting to remain at home was that I had had the privilege of having a full-time mother. Even though I was an only child, my parents had foregone a needed second income so that my mother could stay home with me — cooking good meals, sewing my clothes, being a room mother at school, supervising my practice, transporting me to lessons and classes, helping me with my homework, listening to my problems, and sitting by my side when I was sick. She had always been there for me, and I wanted to pass that on to my children. I realized that it was a luxury in our economy to have the choice to stay home, and I was grateful for the chance.

I was six months pregnant when I returned to the university for the last time to attend my doctoral graduation. A dear friend labeled my name tag: "Dr. Mom." I sat during the ceremony thinking how nice it was to be leaving this pressured life entirely behind. I was looking forward to being home, relaxing with my new baby. How God must have smiled! It was probably the same smile He had when I married my free-spirited husband and thought that we were going to "live happily ever after." God knew that I would never work so hard in my life as when my spunky daughter was born!

"Dr. Mom," my name tag jokingly shouted. Yet this exactly summed up my dilemma. I had one foot in a professional world, where my dissertation research had just been accepted for journal publication, and I had one foot in a world where I wanted to be a full-time wife and mother. The constant jokes about my "getting a doctorate to quit work and stay home to have a baby" were wearing thin. I also realized that taking a break for a few years to raise small children and return to work was a myth. We wanted more children, and I had continually observed that children needed their parents' time just as much or more as they got older and hit the teenage years. I still remember the number of rotating teenage friends who ate meals at my mom's kitchen table because they didn't want to go back to an empty or stressful home.

I was at a turning point in my life. God had clearly led me in two separate life directions, and I didn't see how He could possibly combine them. What was the life's path that He had planned for me? Was it possible to be a "professional" at home? With my little girl as my constant companion, I began a journey of seeking God through His Word to understand the direction He had set before me. This journey of amazing discoveries is what I want to share with you. It is not to be misunderstood as an attack on working women, especially those who work out of financial need. Some of my dearest friends work outside the home! It is dedicated to all women who have shared my journey and seek to be God's professionals on the homefront.

Reality Check

My respect for mothers rapidly increased when I became one! I found my "extensive background" to be quite deficient. In *no* job situation or graduate course was I taught the following:

- Where to put the week's groceries when you have two children in the cart.

- How to carry on an intelligent adult conversation when your new baby has kept you up every night for a month.

- How to be on time to a meeting when your child dirties her diaper at the precise moment that you are putting her in the car seat.

- How to appear halfway professional when your two-year-old still insists on nursing.

- How to drive your older child to school when your toddler has the stomach flu and is certain to decorate the new car.

- How to serve coffee at a meeting that you are leading when your two-year-old has just put peanuts in the coffee grinder.

- How to use the bathroom with a little person sitting on your lap.

- What to do when your three-year-old puts every toy and puzzle piece she owns into the toilet to "teach them to swim."

● How to accompany a choir in public performance when your four-year-old walks up on the stage in the middle of the number and starts "playing a duet with you."

Time for Reflection

1. What have been God's turning points in your life?

2. Do you believe that being a professional woman can be consistent with being at home?

Greet Priscilla and Aquila, my fellow workers in Christ Jesus. They risked their lives for me. Not only I but all the churches of the Gentiles are grateful to them. Greet also the church that meets at their house. Greet my dear friend Epenetus, who was the first convert to Christ in the province of Asia. *Greet Mary, who worked very hard for you.* Greet Andronicus and Junias, my relatives who have been in prison with me. They are outstanding among the apostles, and they were in Christ before I was. Greet Ampliatus, whom I love in the Lord. Greet Urbanus, our fellow worker in Christ, and my dear friend Stachys. Greet Apelles, tested and approved in Christ. Greet those who belong to the household of Aristobulus. Greet Herodion, my relative. Greet those in the household of Narcissus who are in the Lord. *Greet Tryphena and Tryphosa, those women who work hard in the Lord. Greet my dear friend Persis, another woman who has worked very hard in the Lord.*

(Romans 16:3–12, emphasis added)

HARDWORKING WOMEN

C hristian women are intended to be industrious women. With no reflection intended on our fathers, brothers, husbands, and sons, who are singled out in this passage of greetings as being the hard workers? The women!

My first discovery on the homefront was that I had cultural blinders on! I had succumbed to the not-so-subtle battle between professional career women and women who choose to stay home to care for their families. It was portrayed as a black-or-white battle, evidenced especially in the church. A careful study of Scripture revealed a surprising position. The godly woman modeled for us in Scripture is neither "at home" nor "at work," but is an *integration* of the two roles.

Throughout Scripture, reference to women's roles are coupled with directives to be industrious, busy, productive, hardworking, and skillful. Note the often-quoted verse:

Then they can train the younger women to love their husbands and children, to be self-controlled and pure, to be busy at home, to be kind, and to be subject to their husbands, so that no one will malign the word of God. (Titus 2:4–5)

Too many Christian men and women have focused on the "being at home" section of the verse and missed the critical message. Yes, we are to be on the homefront, but we are to be *BUSY* at home. To be busy is to be industrious, diligent, and engaged in working toward a goal. It is a highly productive state. The Greek word used in this passage for "busy" is *oikouros* which means "to guard." To guard is to protect from danger by watchful attention. We are on duty! We are hardworking soldiers on the homefront.

Givers not Takers

Christian men and women are clearly called to be productive people — people who make contributions to those around them. Our witness is rooted in being givers, not takers. We are to embody the opposite of idleness. The best definition of idleness I know is in reference to a motor. A motor which is idling is "running disconnected so that its power is not employed for useful work." Isn't that exactly what idle Christians are doing? They are running disconnected! God's power cannot be channeled for useful work. Their energies serve no purpose. To be industrious is not optional for Christian men *or* women:

> She watches over the affairs of her household and does not eat the bread of idleness. (Proverbs 31:27)

> The way of the sluggard is blocked with thorns, but the path of the upright is a highway. (Proverbs 15:19)

One who is slack in his work is brother to one who destroys. (Proverbs 18:9)

Our people must learn to devote themselves to doing what is good, in order that they may provide for daily necessities and not live unproductive lives. (Titus 3:14)

Avoiding Idleness

We are not commanded to avoid idleness because God is a slavedriver! In addition to being an effective witness, we are commanded to work hard because it is *good* for us. "Idle minds are the devil's playground" is a well-founded saying. Note that idleness breeds poverty, fantasies, and excessive sleep:

How long will you lie there, you sluggard? When will you get up from your sleep? A little sleep, a little slumber, a little folding of the hands to rest — and poverty will come on you like a bandit and scarcity like an armed man. (Proverbs 6:9–11)

He who works his land will have abundant food, but he who chases fantasies lacks judgment. (Proverbs 12:11)

Do not love sleep or you will grow poor; stay awake and you will have food to spare. (Proverbs 20:13)

To engage in a fantasy world and excessive sleep are forms of detaching oneself from reality, the battlefield of life, and can be signs of depression. Poverty is the state of being without sufficient resources. A lack of hard work not only brings physical poverty, but spiritual poverty as well. God intends us to be productive, spiritually healthy people with ample resources to approach life.

Professionalism

In tracing the portrait of the godly, industrious woman through Scripture, I have discovered nine recurring qualities which she portrays. I share them with you as the framework for this book:

1. She is hardworking and productive.

2. She is skilled and specialized.

3. She is balanced and focused on Biblical priorities, which is reflected in all her relationships.

4. She is an organizer and planner.

5. Her image is dignified and encourages respect.

6. She is an enterprising businesswoman and enabling manager.

7. She is generous and philanthropic.

8. She is an evangelist.

9. She is strong and persevering.

These nine qualities can be summed up in one word: The godly woman is a professional. The term *professional* can be offensive because in our society it has come to mean receiving monetary compensation for acquired skills, but that is *not* the original definition of the word:

Professional—one engaged in a calling requiring specialized knowledge and preparation; a principal calling, vocation, or employment.

To be a professional is to be trained, expert, and excellent at one's work. We, as Christian women, are called by God to professionally approach each task He gives us with a dedication to excellence and hard work. Let us discover together how we can be "professionals on the homefront."

Before having children, becoming a "professional homemaker" sounded about as attractive to me as being tarred and feathered at the next church potluck. I never did like the word "homemaking"—until I began investigating its true meaning.

A *home* is defined as: a family unit, a place of origin, a base of operations. To *make* is to create, defined as producing through imaginative skill, such as artwork. The *home* as a place of *origin* is the source at which something begins. From it we derive the word *original*, which means a creative work, not a copy. You as a homemaker essentially create original artwork. Your family has never existed before and will never exist again. Every day you paint another memory in their lives.

Have you ever received a professionally packaged gift in the mail? No matter how fragile the item enclosed or how many bumps the package has endured along the way, the expertly placed layers of tissue paper and foam protect it. A family is like that. Those people are a gift to us. They are fragile. They will receive numerous bumps in life meant to destroy them. But if they are expertly wrapped in layers of unconditional love and support, they will survive.

What is a mom? She is a professional packer — God's packer.

Reality Check

One of my pet peeves is daytime television. Perhaps this stems from seeing even young children in the hospital watch soap operas for hours.

When I had my first child, my hospital roommate watched television from 7:00 A.M. to 11:00 P.M. I didn't say anything because I didn't want to offend her, but one morning she went to take a shower, and I didn't see why I had to watch it when she wasn't even there! So I turned it off. She was not pleased when she returned. I did offend her. She looked at me and said, "This is your first child, isn't it? You've been working." I answered, "Yes." She replied, "You'll see. . . . You'll change." I thought to myself, "I'll change? I'll watch television all day? That's the life of a homemaker? No way!"

Time for Reflection

1. Consider these additional Biblical passages on productivity: Proverbs 21:5, Proverbs 21:25, Proverbs 12:27, 1 Thessalonians 4:11.

2. Review the past week. Which were your most productive times? When did you fall into idleness? Apply the same exercise to the past month and year.

3. Which tasks in your life do you feel you currently approach as a "professional"?

She makes linen garments and sells them,
and supplies sashes for the merchants.

(Proverbs 31:24, NKJV)

THREE

SPECIALIZED WOMEN

I n our society "specialization" connotes professionalism. Does this fit with the Biblical picture of the industrious woman? Yes!

> There are different kinds of gifts, but the same Spirit. There are different kinds of service, but the same Lord. There are different kinds of working, but the same God works all of them in all men. (1 Corinthians 12:4–6)

Godly women are specialized women. Each of us has a unique set of gifts and skills given for the purpose of contributing to God's work. We have spiritual gifts as well as skills, and God intends for them to function as partners.

> Now you are the body of Christ, and each one of you is a part of it. And in the church God has appointed first all apostles, second prophets, third teachers, then workers of miracles, also those having gifts of healing, those able to help others, those with gifts of administration, and those speaking in different kinds of tongues. (1 Corinthians 12:27–28)

The gifts of the Spirit are different from learned skills such as typing, playing an instrument, having computer expertise, and so forth. The ideal match occurs when one's learned skills are the tools of one's gift. For example, one may have the gift of preaching. Skills learned in seminary training, such as fluency in Greek and Hebrew and Biblical scholarship, are the tools. One may have the gift of song combined with fifteen years of studying the piano. Another may have the gift of healing and match that with eight years of medical school! Having a gift is not a license to be lazy in learning to apply it.

Take as an example the godly woman of Proverbs 31. She is an artisan. "She is always busy with wool and flax" (verse 13a, *New Jerusalem Bible*). She "makes her own quilts" (verse 22a, NJB). She "weaves linen sheets and sells them and supplies the merchants with sashes" (verse 24, NJB). We need to diligently develop our skills as well.

In case you have dismissed this in the past, thinking that every woman of this period in history wove her own cloth, look at the clue in verse 24. She sold her goods to the merchants; her products were in demand. The law of supply and demand tells us that her success would not have been possible if every other woman in town was doing the same! This godly woman had a specialization, and she served the community through it. I can also attest that she was highly skilled. As part of my creative arts therapy background, I learned to weave. I can tell you—from winding the warp to warping the loom to planning the colors and patterns to actually weaving the cloth—that weaving is a very long, difficult process. The godly woman of Proverbs 31 is highly skilled in her specialization.

God is not calling all of us to be weavers, but He is encouraging us to develop a specialization, employing our unique combination of gifts and skills to serve Him, our family, and our community. A church community in which each member is sharing his or her special expertise, can far surpass the most efficiently run company!

The Benefits of a Specialization

God's message on skills is especially relevant for our decade. Having a specialization will not only help us serve our community but will help each of us personally. The phenomenon of the eighties is the "mid-life crisis," researched so effectively by Christian authors Jim and Sally Conway. This identity crisis hits Christians as well as non-Christians, men as well as women, especially women who have foregone an education and career to raise families. When the empty nest syndrome sets in and a woman's only life vocation walks out the door when her last child leaves home, she can be headed for a serious depression unless she has other activities in her life. A woman's specialization can be her lifeline when the transitions and crises of life come.

Having an expertise can also provide a much-needed model for our children. There is no question that it is difficult to be a woman in today's world! What message about women's roles are we offering our daughters? I have observed that most young girls fall into two groups upon graduating from high school. Group 1 does not seriously pursue an education or vocation and is seeking to get married and start a family. Group 2 has *no* desire to start a family or be at home any time in the near future and is fully pursuing education and career. I fell into Group 2 as a young girl. I didn't want my mother's life!

Now I have two very bright daughters of my own, and they are filled with potential. How do I motivate them to seek an education and develop a life's vocation and also understand their commitment to a potential future family? I do it by *modeling* an integration of the two roles for them. By my example, I hope to encourage my daughters to seek a professional life — in the work world or on the homefront.

If I have any advice for young girls, it is to obtain all the education, skills training, and job experience they can before marriage, especially before having children. Those are precious years of preparation never to come again. Don't waste them!

The smartest thing my parents and future in-laws did was to ask us not to get married until John finished graduate school and I finished undergraduate school, and we had solid careers. No, we were not pleased! Imagine them ganging up on us like that! How we envied our friends who were so "in love" and getting married as students! Those were the same friends who were getting divorces a few years later.

The Purpose of a Specialization

We must realize that our specialization does not exist for our purposes but for God's purposes. We are a working part of an efficient network designed to bring glory to God, not glory to self.

I can tell you from personal experience that having a specialization is not always enjoyable! I began taking piano lessons at age five. Making music came easily, and by age twelve I was working as an accompanist. I went on to develop many other skills, learned to play other instruments and studied other arts, became a music therapist and music educator, received a seminary degree with an emphasis in pastoral care. But to this day, no matter what activity I am involved in, the leader always turns to me and says, "Oh, good, Mary Ann can play the piano." Sometimes I don't want to play the piano! But I have learned that my gifts were designed for God's purposes, not for my enjoyment. My skills should meet the needs of others; I should not be offering my skills to meet my needs.

I have an excellent example for you. We have dear friends, Greg and Laura, who received intensive training over several years to enter the mission field. Since our church was their major support, they served one year there before leaving to be with their tribe in Papua, New Guinea. When they arrived, all the ministries were fully staffed; there was not even an opening for a Sunday school teacher. The only openings the church had were for a custodian and a typist in the office. Greg cheerfully took the custodian position and Laura accepted the typist position. Many church members criticized them for not utilizing their skills. The question, "How can cleaning toilets prepare one for the mission field?" was often asked. I greatly admired them and knew that they were preparing for ministry in the best way possible. They had the hearts of servants. They saw a need and filled it, regardless of how it reflected on them. The end of the story is that they have been extremely effective ministers to their tribe in Papua, New Guinea. They know how to *serve* the people.

To be a "specialized professional" has nothing to do with the number of degrees you hold, the type and quantity of skills you have, the amount of your salary, or if you even receive a salary. Being a professional, godly woman is to be excellent and expert at employing one's gifts and skills to meet needs.

> Each one should use whatever gift he has received to serve others, faithfully administering God's grace in its various forms. (1 Peter 4:10)

My husband's grandmother wrote a beautiful graduation poem for me when I received my doctorate. Do you know where I hung it? Over my washing machine! Weekly it reminds me that I can be a professional in the most tedious of life's tasks.

The Specialization of Weakness

> Praise be to the God and Father of our Lord Jesus Christ, the Father of compassion and the God of all comfort, who comforts us in all our troubles, so that we can comfort those in any trouble with the comfort we ourselves have received from God. For just as the sufferings of Christ flow over into our lives, so also through Christ our comfort overflows. (2 Corinthians 1:3–5)

Specialization in the secular world is based on achievement and skill. The unique privilege that God's people have is developing a specialization based on weakness and failure. God intends for our heartaches to be the key to helping others.

My greatest weakness is my physical body. I always joke that in heaven I will be an "Amazon woman"—big, strong, and healthy. My earthly life is quite different. I am small, weak, and have suffered with chronic illness problems for years. Depression and emotional discouragement often accompany the condition. But because I know what it is to suffer physically and emotionally, God has built a life's work for me of ministering to other people who hurt. I would not trade those firsthand lessons for anything.

There exists today an abundance of materials to help you analyze your strengths, skills, and temperament. There exist numerous career counseling programs to assist you. These aids are valuable, and a resource list is included in the bibliography. But it is my experience that most women know what their gifts and skills are. For those women I offer a "Time for Reflection" to examine your existing or potential specializations. Remember to not only consider your areas of strength but your areas of weakness and pain as well. Our strongest potential for ministry comes from our weakness. Because of our emotional, physical, mental, or spiritual hurt, we are most capable of helping other people with the same hurt. Perhaps your specialization is leading a support group of people suffering with your same weakness. Perhaps it is praying for, writing to, or visiting people who suffer pain similar to yours. You are the expert because you know what most helps you.

Financial compensation should not influence our choice of a specialization. Depending on our professional specialization, it can be developed as a ministry or a ministry/business. We are no less a professional if we do not charge a fee, and we are no less a minister if we do charge one. We will see in Chapter 9 that the godly woman of

Proverbs 31 was quite a businesswoman, but she remained a minister first.

Reality Check

When I was working and in graduate school, more than one person asked me why I was working so hard. Wasn't it all going to be wasted when I stopped to have a family? Why didn't I stop to have children now and get it over with, and pursue my career later? They made motherhood sound like a prison term, a bad pill to swallow, a time for putting life on hold. Raising a family was posed as the antithesis of growing, learning, thinking, and contributing a specialization.

I have found family life to be quite the opposite. Not only is this the most enjoyable time of my life, but also my children are the most stimulating and challenging teachers I've had yet, and they have tapped every resource in my background.

Time for Reflection

1. Consider and list under different headings your:

   - Spiritual gifts

   - Skills

   - Background and training

   - Interests and hobbies

   - Areas of weakness and pain in your life

   - Activities that you enjoy and activities that you dislike

- Temperament (refer to *Please Understand Me* in the bibliography)

- What needs you are most often asked to meet

- What needs you more often see in others

- What needs you most capably meet in your own family

2. Take some time to review these lists. Look for clues in each area that point toward your potential specializations. Is there one specialization emerging which integrates the ten areas? Refer to the bibliography and Appendix D for a list of professional specialization resources.

We hear that some among you are idle.
They are not busy; they are busybodies.

(2 Thessalonians 3:11)

FOUR

FOCUSED AND BALANCED WOMEN

The godly, industrious woman is *focused.* She concentrates her full attention on her goal without distraction. Her goal is to live a life dedicated to Biblical priorities. She is devoted to doing good (see Titus 3:14). What is the number one Biblical priority? *Relationships.* The productive woman clearly understands the Biblical hierarchy of priority relationships. First, her relationship with God is of ultimate importance. Second, she focuses on her relationship with her husband and children. Third, she focuses on her relationship with the community, from her circle of closest friends to the church to the city to the farthest ends of the mission field.

The essence of hard work is being committed to a relationship. The professional woman of Scripture views productivity and skills as tools in the relationships; they are *not substitutes* for her relationships. Her motto would be "People come first." Her greatest expertise is building relationships. That skill is not optional for God's people.

To be busy is to be contributing constructively, not running around like a chicken with its head cut off! The industrious woman is not a Martha — bustling around in the kitchen instead of investing in relationships. She is a Mary — sitting at Jesus' feet and allowing Him to love others through her. She is ready and equipped to work hard when it serves that purpose.

There is a definite reason that Paul follows the chapter on spiritual gifts in 1 Corinthians with the famous "love chapter," chapter 13. We may have all the gifts and skills in the world, but if they are not channeled in *love*, they are worthless!

Scripturally Balanced

God's professional woman is *balanced*. She is Biblically based. She seriously invests time in a relationship with her Lord, studying His textbook for life, the Bible, and seeking His Kingdom first (see Matthew 6:33). Because she has a grasp of the *entirety* of Scripture, she remains balanced.

Imagine the double-sided scale. When the two scales are in balance, each is in equal proportion to the other. Neither is lopsided at the expense of the other. The balanced woman's view of Scripture is not lopsided. She is focused and balanced in her relationships, her industrious actions, and her speech. She understands the following points of a Biblically-based life.

1. She is a hard worker, but she knows that her work will be in vain if it is not God-centered.

   The blessing of the LORD brings wealth, and he adds no trouble to it. (Proverbs 10:22)

2. She is a planner, but she knows that God is in control of her life and directs her plans.

   To man belong the plans of the heart, but from the LORD comes the reply of the tongue. Commit to the LORD whatever you do, and your plans will succeed. (Proverbs 16:1, 3)

3. She works hard to prepare for the future, but she does not worry about the future. She trusts in God's care.

   She is clothed with strength and dignity; she can laugh at the days to come. (Proverbs 31:25)

   Therefore I tell you, do not worry about your life, what you will eat or drink; or about your body, what you will wear. Is not life more important than food, and the body more important than clothes? Look at the birds of the air; they do not sow or reap or store away in barns, and yet your heavenly Father feeds them. Are you not much more valuable than they? (Matthew 6:25–26)

4. She sees money as a tool for supporting her family and helping others. She does not serve or love money.

   Such people we command and urge in the Lord Jesus Christ to settle down and earn the bread they eat. (2 Thessalonians 3:12)

   People who want to get rich fall into temptation and a trap and into many foolish and harmful desires that plunge men into ruin and destruction. For the love of money is a root of all kinds of evil. Some people, eager for money, have wandered from the faith and pierced themselves with many griefs. (1 Timothy 6:9–10)

We can learn from the Thessalonian church. They were not focused and balanced but were distracted into idleness.

> In the name of the Lord Jesus Christ, we command you, brothers, to keep away from every brother who is idle and does not live according to the teaching you received from us. For you yourselves know how you ought to follow our example. We were not idle when we were with you, nor did we eat anyone's food without paying for it. On the contrary, we worked night and day, laboring and toiling so that we would not be a burden to any of you. We did this, not because we do not have the right to such help, but in order to make ourselves a model for you to follow. For even when we were with you, we gave you this rule: "If a man will not work, he shall not eat."
>
> We hear that some among you are idle. *They are not busy, they are busybodies.* (2 Thessalonians 3:6–11, emphasis added)

This is one of my favorite scriptural messages. Paul did have a sense of humor!

Be Busy Not a Busybody

To be busy is to be constructively contributing to a goal. To be a busybody is to meddle, interfere, and *hinder* progress toward a goal. You can be busy or you can be a busybody, but you cannot be both; they are total opposites! The busybody engages in idle talk and discusses things that are not her place to discuss. She is always in the middle of conflict and controversy. She habitually stirs up trouble, has no self-control, and discourages others from seeking to do good. She is not respected or viewed as trustworthy.

The saddest phenomenon that occurs in the church is when busybodies are given license to operate under the guise of "loving confrontation" and "church discipline." They are *imbalanced* scripturally. They have missed the overall Biblical message of God's unconditional love, acceptance, and forgiveness through Jesus Christ and have become the "spiritual police" on minor issues.

In contrast, the godly professional woman who is focused and balanced knows that "All hard work brings a profit, but mere talk leads only to poverty" (Proverbs 14:23). She is a peacemaker. "She speaks with wisdom, and faithful instruction is on her tongue" (Proverbs 31:26). She is self-controlled. She "avoid[s] foolish controversies and genealogies and arguments and quarrels about the law, because these are unprofitable and useless" (Titus 3:9). She spurs others "on toward love and good deeds" (Hebrews 10:24). She is the oil in God's machinery which helps every working part to run smoothly, harmoniously, and efficiently. The busybody clogs up the machinery.

Reality Check

I became a follower of Jesus Christ as a young adult, so I did not grow up in the church. My first exposure to the body of Christ came as a church musician. I went from no knowledge of Jesus Christ straight to a church staff position as a new convert with my husband. You can imagine my disillusionment over the petty arguments, backbiting, and anger so rampant in the church and so obvious to church staffs who must deal with them. My non-Christian friends never acted like this!

Now as an old veteran of church wounds, I know that there will never be a perfect church because there are no perfect people, and that is why Jesus Christ came to die on the cross.

Out of focus and unbalanced people come to Jesus for healing. I caution you to not fall into the trap of judging the "judgers." Those who stir up conflict often need the most love and tenderness.

Time for Reflection

1. List in order of priority the areas of focus in your life. Do your actions reflect this order? Is a relationship with God your ultimate priority?

2. When do you most easily put people first? When is it most difficult for you?

3. Do you have a balanced view of Scripture? Are there areas that are lopsided?

4. Are you a peacemaker or do you fall into the trap of idle talk and conflict? Are you the encouraging "oil"?

No one who practices deceit will dwell in my house; no one who speaks falsely will stand in my presence.

(Psalms 101:7)

Why do you look at the speck of sawdust in your brother's eye and pay no attention to the plank in your own eye? How can you say to your brother, "Let me take the speck out of your eye," when all the time there is a plank in your own eye? You hypocrite, first take the plank out of your own eye, and then you will see clearly to remove the speck from your brother's eye.

(Matthew 7:3–5)

AVOIDING THE HYPOCRISY SYNDROME

No one wants to be a hypocrite, but since we are all human, we each fall prey to this most devious of Satan's tricks. Satan's favorite device is to turn our priorities upside down. He strives to cloud our focus and push us off balance. The godly professional seeks God first, then cares for her family, and then serves the community. Each is an outflow of the other. But many well-meaning women fall into the trap of serving the community first, then fitting in their family's needs, and finally having a few minutes left over to spend with God. They are always fighting burnout because their resources are constantly running dry. Life is running backwards!

Consider the following "log in the eye" situations:

- Sally teaches gourmet cooking classes two evenings a week. Her family is home eating TV dinners.

- Joan is adamantly against mothers leaving their children to work outside the home. She attends three morning Bible studies a week and leaves her children in nursery care.

- Sue is a successful music teacher. She is based at home and has a large number of students. By the end of the day, she is too tired to give her own children music lessons.

- Kathy diligently prepares and teaches two Bible studies a week. She does not have devotions with her own children.

- Stacy does not have time to clean her home or prepare meals this week because she is attending a "Home Organization Seminar."

- Ann is a successful author. She hasn't written a thank you note or encouraging card to family or friends in weeks.

- Linda is an accountant working at home. At tax time, she is swamped and unable to help her husband with their own taxes.

Scriptural teaching is very clear on this point. As an overflow of our relationship with God, our skills and specialization are designed to professionally serve our family *first.* Our family members are our first customers. They are the first beneficiaries of our gifts. "Her children arise and call her blessed; her husband also, and he praises her" (Proverbs 31:28).

It is no accident that this verse occurs near the end of the eighteen-verse list of this godly woman's commitments. Her husband and sons praise her and call her blessed. They have been her first priority from the beginning and have not suffered for her use of skills. She has brought them "good, not harm, all the days of her life" (Proverbs 31:12).

Priority Safeguards

Each family is different. We must examine the individual needs of our family members. Forty-five-year-old Marie, who has a husband and a twenty-year-old son, has different requirements on the homefront than thirty-year-old Carol, the mother of four preschool children, who has a husband that travels. Carol's specialization may be based entirely at home, concentrating on her children, while Marie may have a thriving business that serves the community. But Carol and Marie are *both* professionals. They approach their life's tasks and serve those around them in a professional manner, employing their skills and gifts. We can certainly have different specializations throughout our lives. Carol may channel her abilities in a totally different direction in fifteen years, but her attitude of professionalism will not change.

Simply being at home is not the critical piece of the puzzle. Staying at home is a choice that I have made, but I would never impose that on other sisters in Christ, especially those who work out of financial need. I have known women who work outside of the home who perfectly match the needs and schedules of their families, and I have known women at home who are absorbed in such a variety of activities that the needs of their families come last. The critical piece of the puzzle is having an *attitude* of guarding the homefront and serving God and family as a top priority.

We must each set guidelines for working as a professional on the homefront. I share with you the guidelines that I, a mother of small children with a husband in a demanding executive position, set seven years ago. They apply to my church and social activities as well. These are the limits that have effectively met the needs of my family and allowed me to professionally serve others. My guidelines may not be your guidelines because your family may have different needs.

I share my specialization when it:

- Involves and benefits my children and husband.

- Does not require me to be separated from my children or husband.

- Does not require my husband to babysit in the evenings.

- Serves people in the community who understand that my family comes first.

- Involves me in church activities which include my husband or children.

Hidden Hypocrisy

There is a second type of hypocrisy which is less obvious and is my weakness. It is a lack of *true* conviction or rather, "Conviction is fine as long as it does not offend anyone." I will do most anything to not cause conflict or offend another party. Ironically my husband subscribes to the opposite viewpoint: "If you're going to accomplish anything, it's going to offend someone. You have to press on." You can imagine that our opposing views have made for some great arguments!

I had one lesson on hypocrisy in graduate school that I will never forget. It was the day of my doctoral oral exams, and I was terrified. I was facing a panel of five professors who could ask me *anything* about their respective fields. (Unless I am well prepared with written notes, I turn into a blithering idiot in front of a group. I mispronounce words and become tongue-tied. I can't think fast on my feet. It is my greatest embarrassment in life.)

God miraculously supported me through the exam, and the last question was asked. I answered it and the professor began questioning if I was correct. I immediately backed down, apologized, and said that I was probably wrong.

My own mentor professor threw his hands up in the air and yelled, "Mary Ann! Don't capitulate! Stand up for what you believe in!" My answer was correct. What was wrong was my unwillingness to fight for it.

That lesson has stayed with me. How many times must God throw His hands up in the air and yell, "Mary Ann! Don't capitulate! Stand up for your convictions!"

Reality Check

I saw this plaque on one of those "off" days with my children. It did tickle my funny bone!

> I love to give homemade gifts . . .
> which one of the kids would you like?

Time for Reflection

1. List the ages and needs of each member of your family.

2. Create a set of guidelines for your activities which matches the needs of your family.

3. Review the potential specialization that you considered in Chapter 3 in light of these guidelines. Which specializations are feasible? Which serve your family first? Which would tempt you into hypocrisy?

4. For what areas of conviction do you struggle standing up?

Commit to the Lord whatever you do, and your plans will succeed.

(Proverbs 16:3)

ORGANIZATION AND PLANNING

I wish there existed a support group for people like me — Organizers Anonymous. The group would probably fail anyway because the members would be too involved in organizing it! I have had the compulsive discipline to organize and plan since I was a small child. I blame my parents first. They were both very organized, hardworking people and consistently modeled it. What chance did I have? They also instilled discipline in me. Whether it was homework, piano practice, or cleaning my room, they required it to be done at the same time every day regardless of circumstances. Illness was the only excuse. So I never learned how to be easily distracted from reaching a goal. They went around saying things like, "Once you start it, you finish it. Never give up," and "If it's worth doing, it's worth doing well."

Things worsened as I got older. They didn't just tell me to do my jobs but were at my side helping me and supplying me with the tools I needed. Unfortunately, they wouldn't settle for mediocrity. They believed that my work could be outstanding.

Even worse, they became involved in organizing my activities. My mother was a Room Mother at school. When I was in Girl Scouts, she was a leader. She got to know my teachers and would even have them to our house for dinner.

They insisted on showing me, through their marriage and friendships, that relationships required the same hard work and commitment as other tasks. Over and over again, they led me down a path of discipline and organization that I could never recover from. For those of you who hope to avoid this syndrome and encourage your children to be disorganized or undisciplined, simply follow these guidelines:

- Do not personally model an organized life for them. The only way they will know how to live a chaotic lifestyle is to experience one at home.

- Do not have a schedule for your children. Encourage them to do their jobs only when they feel like it.

- Let them quit working at tasks when the tasks become difficult. Allow them to be distracted into other areas.

- Do not assist them with their tasks. If they have a school project, don't help them research it at the library. Let them figure it out by themselves.

- Don't expect your children to do their best. Be happy with as little effort as possible. It's not that important in the long run.

- Do not become involved in their activities. You have better things to do with your time.

- If a relationship becomes difficult or inconvenient and is no longer enjoyable, let it go. You can make other friends. If your marriage is experiencing struggles, consider ending it. Don't be so committed to any relationship that it causes you problems or pain.

Our Heavenly Parent

Seriously, I am very grateful to my parents for the valuable training I received from them. But more important, what type of parent is God our Father? Are industrious women the children of a father who encourages organization, discipline, and commitment or disorganization and chaos? God intends for His people to be organizers and planners:

> On the open ground, plan what you have to do, make your preparation in the field; then you may go and build your house. (Proverbs 24:27, NJB)

> Snow may come, she has no fears for her household, with all her servants warmly clothed. (Proverbs 31:21, NJB)

Winter was coming, and the godly woman had already "warmly clothed her household." To prepare for the future is very different from worrying about it; to plan is simply being a wise steward of the resources that God has given us. In fact, God may encourage us to plan because He knows that it is one of the best remedies for worry! Perhaps the woman of Proverbs 31 "laughed at the days to come" because she was prepared for them.

Planning

Having vision is the privilege of the Christian's life. Planning, defined as developing a method for achieving a goal, is a Biblical concept and supports the old adage, "If you fail to plan, you plan to fail." But there is a critical difference between secular planning and a plan based on faith. The plan in the Christian's life is a tool which God directs, changes, and intervenes in. God goes before us to lead us and follows behind to protect us (see Isaiah 52:12). The plan may be modified, radically changed, or discarded, but it has served God's purposes to move the Christian in a positive, constructive, and purposeful direction. It is impossible to go backwards when you are going forward. And Christians are called out to be forward-moving people!

Christians who take the time to plan are certainly not immune to failure, but let us recognize that there are two types of failure in life. First there exists the failure of falling short of a goal that we are trying to reach. That is "good" failure. We have learned and gained from the experiences of trying and will be better equipped for the next task. The second type of failure is tragic. It is the failure of never trying, never setting a goal to reach—tolerating day-to-day survival without ever having raised our eyes to the vision beyond. This is true failure filled with regret.

The opposite of failure is commitment: deliberate action toward a goal. Our goal is the purpose of God, living as a mirror of Jesus Christ. Organization and planning are the tools, not the goal. Upon walking into any bookstore, Christian or secular, you will observe that the American public is obsessed with organizing their life, their time, their household, their appearance, their financial state. We have missed the point! Organization has become the goal instead of the method.

Be clear on this: The goal of this book you are reading now is *NOT* organization. One of the purposes of our journey together is to help you get organized so that you can reach your goal of being an effective minister of the gospel.

Organization, which includes planning, is defined as "arranging parts into a cohesive whole." If you can arrange the pieces of your life into a united effort, you will be on your way to a godly, professional lifestyle.

Reality Check

The best remedy for any compulsive organizer is to get married or, even more foolproof, to have children! My husband is a genius and is also the classic "absent-minded professor"! He can unravel the most complex problem, but he cannot hang up a piece of clothing, rinse a dish, find a trash can, pick up a towel, remember a date on the calendar, or do any other mundane task. He is also a night owl, so our house every morning looks like someone gave a great party the night before! His actions are not malicious; routine tasks are simply beyond him. A very wise woman told me early in my marriage that I could try and change my husband's habits, but I would lose much more than I would gain. I would become his mother and lose a friend. Over a decade later, my husband and I are still friends, and I schedule a good chunk of my morning to pick up after him. That's reality!

Creative children are another source of cure for the organizer! From Playdoh, chalk, and paint on the floor to sand from the sandbox to "reorganized" drawers and clos-

ets to multicolored outfits, life is never the same. My old-
est daughter's most creative effort occurred when she took
a skein of yarn and wrapped it through the entire house to
make her own "spiderweb."

My favorite grandmother, another compulsive organizer, never remarried after her husband died and her son
was raised. She said that "people confused one's life." I
thank God that families are not convenient and do confuse
our lives. Let us view our organization systems as tools to
help our families, not see our families as enemies of our
organization systems.

> Cleaning and scrubbing can wait till tomorrow
> 'Cause babies grow up, we've learned to our sorrow.
> So quiet down cobwebs, and dust go to sleep,
> 'Cause I'm rocking my baby and babies don't keep.
> 'Cause I'm rocking my baby and babies don't keep.
>
> (Folk Song)

Time for Reflection

1. Do you "overorganize" or "underorganize"?

2. What are your visions and plans for the next week?
   month? year? your life?

A friend loves at *all* times.

(Proverbs 17:17a, NKJV)

SEVEN

DEVELOPING YOUR ORGANIZATION SYSTEM

D evising organization systems is big business! Seminars, books, and other materials for organizing the time and resources of every profession — corporate executive to homemaker — are found everywhere.

The problem is that each of us perceives the world and processes information differently. Some of us are visual learners; others are auditory learners. Some of us break down a whole concept into parts easily but struggle with disjointed pieces. Others are overwhelmed by the "whole" and work readily from "puzzle pieces" toward the goal. The point is that organization systems must be individualized. Many people grab onto the latest popular organization system and then feel like failures when it doesn't work for them. The person who designed that system may "think differently" from the person who purchased it.

You have two options in choosing your system of organization: find a system that matches your pattern of thinking (perceiving and processing), or create your own system.

All organization systems have one factor in common: they break down an ultimate goal into smaller goals that are reachable on a daily basis. For example, at one time (pre-children!) I was attending two separate graduate programs simultaneously in addition to working two jobs. I was presented with two wonderful educational opportunities, and I couldn't pass up either one, so I did both. Yes, I had lost my mind! You can imagine that the reading load was overwhelming. I applied my "break-down system" and survived. I divided the number of pages in each book by the number of days in the semester. Ten thousand pages of reading was overwhelming, so I broke it down to fifty-five pages a day. I could handle that! The system can be applied to *any* activity.

I am going to share with you my organization system as an example of what any good system should include. I do not recommend that you employ the system personally. Simply use it as a model to design your own system. What materials you use are not important. You may choose notebooks, listpads, index cards, file boxes, or any other products. The organization principles remain the same.

The System
Professional Attitude

The first thing you must do in developing an organization system is to view yourself as the *professional, specialized* woman that God has made you. You must have a professional attitude. For the remainder of this book, you should see yourself as the founder of a company, a company dedicated to God's purposes. Your time is the "president's time," and your home is the "office and warehouse."

Imagine doing business with the following company:

The president comes to work in his pajamas. His office is a mess. You try to make an appointment to see him, but he doesn't have an appointment calendar. He doesn't operate his company on a schedule. His motto is, "Eventually the work gets done." You try to purchase some of the company's products. The warehouse is so disorganized that he can't find them. His shelves are stocked with ten-year-old, outdated merchandise, so he has no room for the new merchandise. He failed to order one of the products you are requesting. He has no system for staying in touch with or thanking his customers. His employees have no idea what products they are handling or what the goals of the company are. There is no profit-sharing since there are no profits! He has no plans for the future growth of the company. His other motto is, "Get the job done with minimal effort. We just want to survive, not be the best."

Would this company succeed in the business world? Neither does such a company succeed on the homefront!

A successful company is an efficiently run company. Efficiency can be defined as "productivity without waste." The opposite of waste is "make the most of every opportunity" (Colossians 4:5b).

Reference and Calendar Books

In my earlier years I put myself in the terrible position of not having one spare minute. I do not recommend it! A foolproof organization system was not a luxury; it was necessary to my survival. My brain could simply not hold all the information. I began by compartmentalizing the dif-

ferent areas of my life: this job, that job, the church ministry, this graduate program, that graduate program, our personal life and household, our social life, and so on. I developed a planning notebook for each area, with tabbed
sections for further breaking down the demands. Each
would include: projects in process (short-term goals), future projects (long-term goals), and Master Lists.

These were my "reference books." Then I had my calendar book which I always kept with me in my purse. It
included: my daily calendar, my overall year calendar, and
a smaller notebook for lists of immediate goals (a "Things
to Do List"). For each reference notebook, there corre-
sponded a page in the "To Do" book listing what I needed
to do for the week. I was *only* responsible each week for
what was written on that notepad — not for eight notebooks
full of tasks.

One day at work I had my purse stolen. I didn't care
about the money, my credit cards, my keys, . . . but what
would I do without my calendar notebook? I couldn't remember where I was supposed to be the next hour, much
less the next week! I was devastated. A few days later,
Security recovered my purse with everything in it *except
my calendar!* What was a thief going to do with my lists?!
I realized that God was giving me a very clear message: it
was all right to be organized, but He was in control of my
life. Organization was a tool, not an object of worship.

Master Lists

Goal targeting was only half of the puzzle. The critical
part was organizing the routine aspects of life so that I

could focus on my goals. The tool was the "Master List," and its concept could be applied to any task.

One type of Master List was a Supplies List of what I needed to have in stock. There was a list for every room in the house and every activity. For example, there was a Bathroom Supplies list, a Kitchen Supplies list (including food items), a Guest Room Supplies list, a Gift/Card Center Supplies list, a Cleaning Supplies list, and so on. When I went marketing, I simply looked at my Kitchen and Bathroom Master List to write down quickly what I needed to purchase. When guests were coming for a visit, I consulted my Guest Room list to restock the room.

Guest Room Master List

- Clean sheets and towels, extra blankets
- Fresh flowers
- Maps and tourist information
- Stationery, books, magazines
- Cold drinks, mints, other snacks
- Cups, hot pot, coffee, tea, hot chocolate mixes, napkins
- Candles
- An extra key
- Toiletries: Kleenex, toilet paper, extra toothbrush, hand cream, etc.

The reason for having Master Supply Lists was that I had no time to go shopping! I needed to make one to two lengthy shopping trips a month versus several short trips a week. I also made use of high quality catalog companies to order by mail. When a friend was sick, there was no time in my day to pick up a Get Well card.

Gift/Card Center List

Cards: Children/Adult Birthday, Get Well, Encouragement/Friendship, Sympathy, New Home, Bon Voyage, Anniversary, New Baby, Thank You, Congratulations, Wedding.

Stationery: Invitations, ribbon, wrapping paper, stickers, banners, balloons, gifts on hand, calligraphy/lettering pens, mailing tape, paper and envelopes, stamps, boxes, bags, baskets.

The Master Lists applied to tasks as well as supplies. For example, a Cleaning List listed each separate task required to keep my house clean: weekly, monthly, and every six months ("spring cleaning").

This system organized information as well. For example, I kept a recipe book which listed every recipe I had by category and where it was located (card file, book, etc.). We often had guests for dinner. Instead of rummaging through my recipe file, I would glance at my Recipe Master List to select the dishes I would serve. This system also made for fast home menu planning each week.

The Idea Book

Another piece of the puzzle was the "Idea Book"—a pocket-size notebook that I kept with me always. The reason for the Idea Book was that I had a terrible memory!

Information would come in one ear and fly out through the other if I didn't *write it down*. The Idea Book was simply to jot down my thoughts and incoming information: a brainstorm for next year's research, the news that Sally had her baby or Tina was sick, a new recipe to try, an idea for a class I was teaching, a gift idea, or an address for a newcomer at church. I could act on the information later.

Filing

The next aspect of any organization plan is the filing system. Between my husband and me, the amount of paper work that came through our home was overwhelming! In two or three days without filing, we would be knee-deep in projects, bills, professional journals, personal and professional correspondence, and tax records. To combat this, I kept a two-fold filing system: permanent filing and temporary filing.

The temporary filing system was a fabric holder I made with nine separate pockets. It hung out of sight on the inside of the kitchen pantry door. Every piece of paper that came into our house was filed immediately into one of the pockets, labeled, for example, church activities, household, bills, or to file permanently.

The subjects kept changing as our activities changed. When we acted on information in any of the pockets, it was thrown away (e.g., directions to a party) or put in the "To File" pocket (e.g., tax receipts). Once a month I permanently filed in our cabinets the "To File" papers.

Today I also enjoy using bulletin boards covered in decorative fabrics for phone messages, a family calendar, cards from friends, pictures, holiday decorations, invitations, and other memorabilia. I have one in my kitchen, my work room, and each of my children's rooms.

Scheduling

Having a routine schedule is critical to organization. A daily schedule may include Bible study, exercise, and meal preparation. A schedule is different from a calendar of activities. A schedule, our outline of weekly chores, sets the routine tasks of life in place so that we can be involved in other activities. A weekly Chore Schedule may look like this:

Monday:	Correspondence/paper work/menu planning
Tuesday:	Marketing and errands
Wednesday:	Housecleaning
Thursday:	Laundry
Friday:	Project Day
Saturday:	Yard
Sunday:	Hospitality Day

It may surprise you to know that very organized, efficient women are usually *NOT* immaculate. They are neat and know where everything is. Their drawers and closets are orderly. They are basically clean and schedule to clean their house one day a week. But they realize that if one is always going to have an immaculate house, it needs to be recleaned every day! They have other goals in life besides a freshly cleaned house. They keep their house up daily but not at the expense of reaching more important goals.

It is also a fact that creativity makes a mess. Anyone who sews, cooks great meals, or attempts any major project knows that there is a huge mess to clean up afterward! Artistic children make especially big messes.

While I was leading a children's group in making collages, one youngster said, "But Mrs. Froehlich, we are making a mess." I answered, "Of course! You can't create art without making some kind of a mess." He looked at me bewildered. Obviously this was not a popular viewpoint in his home! It always saddens me when my children's friends are thrilled to paint and play with clay at our kitchen table because "their mommies don't let them at home."

Professional women are certainly not slobs, nor is their work an excuse for that. They are neat and clean but not fanatical at the expense of people's needs and long-range projects.

Work Center

"Work Centers" are the next piece of the puzzle. For each activity you do, you should have a work center or "office" with all the materials you need at your fingertips. The kitchen is the work center for cooking. A desk is the work center for correspondence. A closet may be the work center for craft projects. My living room is my Music Room/Work Center for teaching. My work centers have ranged from briefcases to drawers to shelves.

When my husband recently converted our attic into a library/office for himself, he gave me the back corner of the attic. I was fortunate enough to gain a project room for my work center. But it is not important if your Work Center is half a closet or an entire room as long as it is conducive to *working*. Your most important work center will be developed for your specialization.

Retreat Planning Time

Since our organization system is based on preparation, we must build into our schedule *time to plan*. We should allow an hour to plan for the week, ideally on Monday. We should allow two hours to plan for the month, ideally at the first of the month. We should even reserve one full day for planning for the year, ideally in January (or August/September if you operate on a school year). These planning retreats should enable seeking God's direction as a first priority and channeling it into goals and priorities.

"The People Book"

I have saved the most important part of the system for last. This is where most organizational systems fall short. Remember that "people come first" for the godly professional woman. Organization systems exist to help us reach goals. If ministering to people as a reflection of Jesus Christ is our ultimate goal, then we should certainly not stop now in applying our system to the area of relationships! This is where it is needed the most and will do the most good.

Don't think of this as a cold "system for organizing relationships" but as a "process for nurturing relationships." Jesus had a plan for reaching the world through His disciples, His public speaking, His visitations, and other activities. He was organized and goal-directed. God certainly had a plan for our redemption. To be organized to care for people is Biblical and is your first priority.

No task is more important than caring for people. What did it matter if I published my doctoral research if I forgot Lisa's birthday? What did it matter if I completed my seminary degree if I didn't take Sue a meal when she was sick? What did it matter if I was giving a solo recital if I didn't write a thank you note to Janet for having us for dinner? What did it matter if I received a promotion at work if I didn't invite the new couple at church for dessert?

Building relationships through meeting needs is the greater achievement. There are three aspects of caring for people's needs through valuing them: (1) remember them, (2) appreciate them. and (3) love them unconditionally. This is the foundation of any ministry to Christians or non-Christians.

We can begin this process by making a Master List of our different relationships (an address book is a good place to start):

- Family
- Extended family
- Close circle of friends
- Church family
- Neighbors
- Community friends
- Acquaintances
- Work friends
- School friends

Another view could be:

- Contact daily
- Contact weekly
- Contact monthly
- Send yearly birthday gift
- Send yearly Christmas card

Another view:

- Family
- Out-of-town relatives
- Neighbor friends
- Friends in town
- Friends in another state
- Overseas missionaries
- Long-distance relationships

The point of these lists is to not forget anyone. To be forgotten is the most despairing of human experiences.

Our People Book also includes:

1. A page for each month listing birthdays, anniversaries, graduations, holidays, any opportunity to remember someone. At the end of the month simply glance at the next month's list and transfer to your "To Do" pad. (Don't forget those first of the month birthdays.) Continue adding to the lists. If a baby is born, write down the date to remember the birthday next year. Remember

sad times as well as joyous times. Write down the date of deaths. I can tell you from my grief counseling experience that the first year anniversary of the death is when the family needs the most support and feels very alone.

2. A "Hospitality List" of people that you would like to have into your home.

3. A list of people you would like to get to know.

4. A list of people's hobbies, interests, favorite colors, etc., for choosing gifts.

5. Your Christmas card list.

6. Your Christmas gift list.

7. Correspondence list of thank you notes, letters of response, support cards (friendship, get well, etc.) to send. This is our method for appreciating others. Just as one method of organization is not for everyone, one method of appreciation is not for everyone. Some people are writers so they write easily. Some people are more verbal so they make a phone call easily. The method is unimportant as long as you have a system for appreciation.

8. List of the family traditions you are developing — special days in your husband's and children's lives.

People Come First

Every time you discover a new aspect of nurturing relationships, add it to the People Book. Loving others unconditionally, the essence of the gospel, is the result of being there to support people, remembering them and appreciating them, no matter the circumstances. Commitment is the goal of our People Book.

Just as our specialization focuses on our family first, so should our nurturing method focus on our husband and children and then overflow to others. Look for every opportunity to remember them. Some wives pack surprises in their husband's lunchpails. I enjoy sending cards to my husband's office and hiding presents in his suitcase for business trips. Children's lunches are the perfect place for love messages. The possibilities are endless.

I had the opportunity to test my "People come first system" in a secular college class that I taught. This class was the final course for Senior therapy students graduating into their internships. It included a demanding curriculum of field work, therapy session planning, exams, research papers, and numerous projects. On the first day of class, in covering the requirements for the semester, I explained that their true final exam would occur on the last day of class. I privately gave each student the name of another student in the class. They were to observe the special needs of that student during the semester and bring a gift on the last day of class to meet those needs. The assignments remained secret until the final exam. The students understood why this particular project was the most important: What did it matter if they were the most knowledgeable, caring therapists out in the world if they couldn't care about their own classmates? Seeing and meeting needs starts with the people around you. The final exam was a great success; my students evidenced true caring in action for each other.

The System on the Homefront

I naively thought that when I became a wife and mother at home, I would have much more free time and could discard my system. You veteran mothers know that I soon learned that the homefront job allowed no spare time either! My time was more flexible but not freer. I modified the system; notebooks for my specialization, children, and home projects substituted for work and school notebooks, but the process remained intact.

If my system is overwhelming to you, there is a good reason for that. I did not sit down and write it in a weekend. It developed over a period of years. Do not adopt it unless it exactly fits your personal approach to life. Rather use it as a guide for developing your own system which should include a:

- Professional attitude.

- Process for defining long-term goals, broken down into short-term goals, broken down into immediate daily and weekly tasks (Reference Notebooks).

- Calendar.

- Master List of needed supplies and chores.

- Process for jotting down ideas and information immediately (Idea Book).

- Filing system (temporary and permanent).

- Schedule of weekly tasks.

- Variety of work centers.

- Retreat Planning time.

- Process for nurturing relationships (People Book).

Reality Check

Five Major Time-Wasters:

1. Standing in lines. Do your banking by mail. Buy stamps in bulk and invest in a postal scale to weigh packages. You can eliminate those post office trips. Use shopping catalogs.

2. Engaging in fantasy. Avoid daytime television, romance novels, or any activity which encourages you to dwell in a fantasy world and avoid the "nitty gritty" of life.

3. Excessive sleep. If you take naps, make them short. Long naps can make you feel more lethargic.

4. Repeated shopping trips. Stock up on supplies once or twice a month. Eliminate "picking up a few things."

5. Waiting at doctor's appointments, children's lessons, etc. Pack a bag of "things to do" while waiting: correspondence, craft projects, etc. That time is a gift. Don't waste it.

In ending this section on organization, let us also define what does *not* waste your time: any activity that nurtures relationships or refreshes you. For example:

- Rocking your child to sleep.

- Picking flowers with your children.

- Relaxing in front of your favorite TV show with your husband.

- Reading a good book.

- Taking a short nap.

- Reading stories as a family.

- Singing around the piano together.

- Going out for coffee with a friend.

- Swimming in the pool.

- Going to the mountains for the weekend.

Time for Reflection

1. How do you more easily process information?

2. What organizational materials would you be most comfortable with? (notebooks, cards, lists, etc.)

3. Develop an organization system to enable efficient planning. Use any part of my system (outlined above) that applies to your situation. Refer to the bibliography for a list of organizational resources. You will find an outline of Task Lists in Appendix A.

A good name is more desirable than great riches; to be esteemed is better than silver or gold.

(Proverbs 22:1)

EIGHT

THE PROFESSIONAL IMAGE

The godly professional woman has an "image" of dignity and respect:

> She is clothed in fine linen and purple. (Proverbs 31:22b)

> She is clothed with strength and dignity. (Proverbs 31:25a)

She has a professional image. Before we cringe at the connotation which "professional imaging" holds in our society, let us observe the true definition of the word. *To image* is to reflect, mirror, or represent. Since a professional is one in a specialized calling, professional imaging for us is reflecting the excellent high calling of God. As Christians, we have the privilege of mirroring the One who has called us.

Biblical imaging and secular imaging are similar in that the goal of each is to communicate success and excellence and encourage confidence. The radical difference between them is the measure of success. The world's measure for success is material wealth. If you drive a Mercedes, dress in expensive suits, and live in an exclusive neighborhood, you communicate to your clients that you are very good at what you do. You encourage confidence and trust in your business.

We are to communicate the same message of *spiritual wealth*. We are rich spiritually in our relationship with God and its overflow of love and service to others. Our image — our reflection of God — should encourage others to have confidence in Him, too.

The next aspect of spiritual imaging is to realize that our image reflects on our families as well as God. Note the adjacent verse of Proverbs 31:

> She is clothed in fine linen and purple. Her husband is respected at the city gate, where he takes his seat among the elders of the land. (verses 22b–23)

This godly woman's appearance contributed to her husband's receiving respect. Developing a dignified image is one way that we can love and benefit our families.

We can create a professional image of dignity and respect through these tools: our appearance and our home.

Professional imaging is a visual presentation to those around you. My wise mother used to say, "It's true that you can't tell a book by its cover — but if you don't like the cover, you probably won't take the time to open the book."

Our Appearance

Since the American public is obsessed with "body worship," focusing too much on one's appearance, let us establish a balanced Biblical view from the outset:

> Your beauty should not come from outward adornment, such as braided hair and the wearing of gold jewelry and fine clothes. Instead, it should be that of your inner self, the unfading beauty of a gentle and quiet spirit, which is of great worth in God's sight. For this is the way the holy women of the past who put their hope in God used to make themselves beautiful. (1 Peter 3:3–5a)

Observe these two examples:

> Lynn is a real beauty. God has gifted her with a beautiful face, figure, charismatic personality, and the ability to dress effectively. She is always meticulously groomed and impressively dressed. Her appearance is a palette of artistry. When she walks into a public place, everyone in the room turns around to look at her. Her trademark is a finely pressed suit with perfectly matched accessories. Clients seek to do business with her based on her appearance. They tell her that if "she can do such an expert job at her appearance, then she must do an equally expert job in her business." She is a "winner."

> Even before she became bent from age and toil she had been only five feet tall. Her broad, strong face is deeply lined, and she has taken on the wispy, papery look of the old. But she is nevertheless, commanding. Her blue eyes are steady, authoritative but kind. Her hands and feet are large, knobby, with big joints — the hands and feet of an old working person who has scrubbed many a

floor. (From Tower, C., "Mother Teresa's Work of Grace," *Reader's Digest,* page 168, December, 1987.)

Lynn is an actual woman. Her personal life is as tattered and torn as her appearance is beautiful. She lives a life separated from God and suffers the consequences.

The woman in the second example is Mother Teresa. Her appearance is the least of her concerns.

Who is the "winner"?

Caution #1:

Appearances, the way that we care for the bodies that God has given us, are important, but they are *deceiving.* We can work on our appearance as a reflection of our love for God and our family, but we should never use appearance as a standard for judging others. An insidious thing happens to human beings who work on one aspect of their being: they begin using it as a measuring stick for judging others. If your appearance is too important to you, it is probably too important in viewing others. The balanced woman does not *focus* on appearance in herself or others.

Caution #2:

Now we come to the theme of this chapter. An activity of imaging (exercising, dressing well, painting your house, etc.) is only effective if you do it *for ministry,* not instead of ministry. Balanced women use their image as one of their tools to reach higher goals; they are not obsessed with their image. Their image is not the goal. Their schedule does *NOT* look like this:

Monday:	Run three miles, exercise class
Tuesday:	Work out at gym, have hair cut
Wednesday:	Run three miles, exercise class
Thursday:	Work out at gym, have nails done
Friday:	Run three miles, exercise class
Saturday:	Tanning salon

As a young person in high school, I was as vain as any teenager. One of my "idols" was my nails. They were quite long and I painted them religiously. My piano teacher at the time was very tenderhearted and allowed me to keep them. (Long nails make correct piano technique impossible.) Then I began studying with a very serious piano teacher from Julliard in order to groom me for college. During the first lesson she said, "The nails go or I go!" My nails?! They were my identity with my peers! My mother wisely said, "You can choose vanity or you can choose being useful, but you can't have both in life." I cried and cried as my mom cut my nails to nothing. Then came the cutting remarks from my peers about "how ugly my hands looked." It was time to be useful despite the world's view. As a harpist, my "favorite" commercial on TV is one advertising nail polish through the hands of a harpist displaying her long beautiful nails. It is also impossible to play the harp with long nails! This ad demonstrates worldly deception at its best. Our appearance should serve the useful purposes of God, not hinder them.

This distortion even occurs in the church. I was sitting in church one Sunday morning, lost in thought over my favorite patient who had just died of leukemia, when the

Women's Bible Study leader came to the platform. She announced that the women were meeting to "have their colors done" that week. Since I worked with terminally ill children in a children's hospital, I often had to work hard to focus on someone's latest haircut or dress or their new carpeting since it seemed so irrelevant in contrast to the deep pain that I saw every day. But this announcement hit me particularly hard. It struck me that people were dying and suffering, and the women of our church were spending their time giving fashion seminars! Where had we lost touch with the purposes of God?

In contrast, my employer at the children's hospital taught me that we should be concerned with external appearances for the *right reasons*. Sick children and their families needed the best and should enjoy being in the hospital as much as possible. An attractive and happy environment would enhance their rehabilitation. Our facilities were bright, colorful, and beautifully designed. Uniforms were discouraged and we were asked to dress attractively to present a bright, hopeful image of the hospital.

Image of Appearance

Similarly, we should create a joyous, attractive image of our professional life of faith. We can do this in four ways:

1. *We should care for our bodies.* Wellness programs abound in hospitals and fitness centers to help us maintain good health. The central tools of good health are eating a balanced diet, regular exercise, getting plenty of rest, and avoiding excessive stress. The well-known saying, "If you put a new paint job on a broken-down car, it

is still a broken-down car," is a perfect analogy for our bodies. Working toward good health is where we start.

2. *We should be well groomed.* Our appearance should be neat and clean. This takes time, so build it into your schedule.

3. *We should dress attractively.* Being attractive is the process of attracting others to be with you. You should have a "wardrobe repertoire" for the different aspects of your professional life, to be attractive to adults or children. View yourself as an artist and be aware of fashion trends and what colors and styles become you. You can refer to C. Jackson's *Color Me Beautiful* as a starting point in developing your distinct style and color palette. Enjoy coordinating accessories that will complete your image picture. I actually recommend that you "have your colors done"! You will appear happier and more approachable in becoming colors. Simply don't substitute it for the process of ministry.

4. *We should be dressed appropriately for our work.* Your appearance should be functional. For example, if you are giving a lecture in the community about your specialization, you should dress in business-like fashion. If you are working with young children all day, an elegant business suit is not appropriate. You need to be attractive to the *child* and perhaps should dress casually in bright, fun colors with interesting graphics.

Our Homes

Our home environment is the next facet of our visual presentation. As an extension of our appearance, the same basic principles of design, color, and balance apply. As a creative arts therapist, I had the privilege of gaining some background in art and design. I learned that those principles can apply to how we dress, design a room, set a table, arrange a vase of flowers, arrange a meal, or plan our yard. Artistry can add flair to any task that we face. Even if you do not have an artistic bent, you may want to explore learning these skills. A visit to the library to look at art and design resources is a good place to start.

Between her linen sheets, sashes, and handmade quilts, the woman of Proverbs 31 must have had a beautiful home. The godly professional woman's home is her "office" and her yard is the "grounds." She works at creating a beautiful environment which is neat, attractive, and will make her family and visitors feel comfortable. Many businesses try to create a "home-like environment" to make their customers feel comfortable. The professional on the homefront has the advantage of starting there! Your home should be as individual and unique as you are. It should reflect your distinct priorities and specialization. Make it your signature.

Skill is much more important than money in designing an environment. We have all been in homes which hold several expensive pieces of furniture but evidence no artistry. We have also been in homes which are artistically designed without an abundance of material wealth. Painting one wall in the *right* color can be more effective than buying the wrong set of furniture or rewallpapering the entire house with the wrong paper.

Let your home reflect our God, who is the Master Artist and Designer of Creation. Where He is glorified, there will be true beauty and true art.

Visual Packaging

Our professional image is completed with visual packaging. If your specialization has developed into a business, visual packaging is a necessity. You should have business cards and letterhead stationery printed for all correspondence. If desired, you can name your business and have a graphic artist design a logo to represent its uniqueness. You may want to invest in a brochure explaining your specialized business, philosophy, and credentials. Every contact you have with clients should be professional and visually attractive.

If your specialization is your professional ministry, you should still consider visually packaging your approach to create an identity. There is no reason that you cannot have letterhead stationery for your "home office," with simply your name and address, or "caring cards." If you are an artisan but do not wish to sell your goods, explore creating a name and logo to label your gifts for friends. If you are an excellent cook, have labels custom-made for your dishes, for example, homemade jams. There is no activity that cannot be treated in a professional manner. The ladies on our church prayer chain proved this when they designed this business card to be placed in every pew:

"Cast your burden upon the Lord, and He will sustain you" (Psalm 55:22).

FIRST BAPTIST PRAYER CHAIN

Call Debbie (373–1210)
or Jana (376–1172)

All requests are confidential

The prayer chain is now respected as a professional ministry of the church and is reaching many more people. Professional imaging, reflecting our God and the ministry that He has called us to, is dignified by our appearance, home, and visual package when we cultivate it *for* the ministry, not *instead of* the ministry.

Reality Check

Can mothers create a dignified image? Before I had children of my own, I wondered why most full-time mothers looked so drab — with no flair, no accessories. Motherhood has taught me that if one wears jewelry or scarves, they will be eaten. If one wears elegant shoes, they will be stepped on. If one wears beautiful clothes, they will be spit up on or smeared with peanut butter or chocolate. If one has her nails done, the baby will chew them. If one has a new hairstyle, it will be played with. I learned in design courses that artistry is functional as well as beautiful. The only functional outfit I know of for motherhood is a combat suit!

My most humiliating moments regarding my appearance consistently occur when I have been up all night with a sick child and I run to the pharmacy in the morning to get the needed medication. One young saleswoman even said to me, "My husband and I have been thinking of having children but I am so afraid to look like you." Sometimes women look their worst when they are serving the most. Having observed mothers sitting with their dying children, I know well this fact of ministry.

The appearance of our homes and our visual package also suffer when God directs us in more urgent ministries.

Our "image" is never more important than the love of God we are trying to reflect.

Time for Reflection

1. What "image" have you created in your appearance? Your home? Your visual package?

2. What image would more effectively fit your professional specialization and calling?

Refer to the bibliography and Appendix D for a list of imaging resources. You will find an overview of art and design principles in Appendix B.

She makes linen garments and sells them,
and supplies the merchant with sashes.

(Proverbs 31:24)

She considers a field, and buys it; out of
her earnings she plants a vineyard.

(Proverbs 31:16)

NINE

ENTERPRISING BUSINESSWOMEN

The woman of Proverbs 31 is an enterprising business-woman. She is not only successful at selling her specialization to the community but she knows how to invest her returns. She is a *good* businesswoman. In contrast to the teaching I've received in conservative churches, I see nowhere in Scripture where the verses on being productive and contributing support are limited to men. The woman of Proverbs 31 is a professional businesswoman on the homefront. She is an entrepreneur.

> *Entrepreneur*—one who organizes, manages, and assumes the risks of an enterprise (purposeful project).

At the risk of sounding blasphemous in this decade, I must admit to you that I would have been happy to live in a previous century where women didn't handle money. Numbers and money simply do not interest me. (Fortunately I am married to a master in this area.)

Developing Your Business

"Business" was a negative word to me for years. I was a therapist and a teacher; I cared about people. I loved the arts. The business of "making money" seemed to be the antithesis of that purpose. In the process of developing my part-time home practice, my businessman husband advised me to read the current business literature. I was surprised to learn that good business had much more to do with helping people and striving to make quality contributions to the community than with money and finances, and there were numerous Biblical parallels. Financial gain was simply the natural by-product of a successful, caring business.

"Business" can be defined as:

An activity concerned with supplying and distributing a commodity (valuable and useful service or product).

It usually includes, but does not require, charging a fee. Good business practices are applicable to your life whether you are making money or not. From a business standpoint, your professional specialization may follow three different routes:

1. *Ministry.* Your specialization ministers to those around you and would be harmed by charging a fee. You are similar to a mission organization. Such an organization is an expertly run business, but missionaries do not charge their clients, the people they are evangelizing. They are supported by donations. They are a nonprofit organization. Perhaps your professional life on the homefront is a nonprofit organization supported by your husband. You are a missionary.

2. *Ministry/Business.* Your specialization is primarily a ministry, but the expenses are so great to run your ministry you are required to charge a fee. You are simply covering your overhead. This is my situation. I am a music teacher/music therapist in private practice. I have a substantial amount of cost in my business: music, instruments, professional memberships, to name a few. I only charge enough to cover my expenses. I also offer classes as part of our church program for no cost. If I did not charge, I could not offer this ministry. I also do not feel that it is fair to ask my husband to support this program.

3. *For-Profit Business.* Here you need to make a living to support your family. It is a choice between developing your own business on the homefront or going to work. Certainly you remain a minister first.

Whatever situation is yours, you are still a businesswoman. View your professional specialization as a business and apply the following steps in developing it:

Step 1: Excellence

Your product or service must be excellent, the highest quality possible. There is no point in promoting a mediocre product. God's products are *not* mediocre! You must be customer-centered and do what best serves the client, not what is more convenient for you. You should be familiar with Tom Peters' book on excellence in business, *A Passion for Excellence.* Temper his focus on business with the fact that our families are our first clients. For example, my children are my first students in my music program.

Step 2: Setting Direction

Choose one aspect of your specialization to start with. Your business must have a focused direction. To set that direction, your business plan employs the same planning and organizational principles of setting long-range and short-term goals that we discussed in Chapter 6. Your business/specialization plan should be an extension of your professional life plan.

Step 3: Professional Imaging

The same principles of communicating professionalism through your appearance, home office, and visual package that we discussed in Chapter 8 apply here. Working on one's visual presentation is a key point in any successful business.

Step 4: Promotion

Once the program is conceived and visually packaged, next begins the process of promoting and marketing your expertise to the public. The best promotion in most businesses is word-of-mouth. The excellence of your work speaks for itself. But if you are just starting out in your business, you should consider the following promotional ideas:

- The most basic advertisement is in the local newspaper, community bulletin, or Yellow Pages.

- You can direct mail your brochure to select groups with a letter introducing yourself. Enclose a postcard that they can return to you if they would like more information and then you can contact them by phone. Post your brochure at preschools if your specialization targets preschoolers; at Senior Citizen Centers if your specialization targets the aging, etc. Make sure that the right population is receiving your information.

● Offer to give lectures on your specialization to relevant community groups with potential clients.

● Offer to teach an introductory class in your expertise as a free community service for children or adults at a facility such as a recreation center, community school, or church. This would be an ongoing feeder program which would constantly introduce new clients to you.

The transition from inquiry to client should be handled in a professional manner also. If the inquiry is a phone call, send a personal letter with your brochure. If you promote your business intelligently, you will probably have more clients than you have time for.

Step 5: Maintaining Your Business

The only way to maintain an excellent program is to diversify and expand. If a business is not growing in new ways, it will eventually become stale and go backward. Innovation and vision are the best remedies for burnout. Do not load your schedule so full with clients that you have no time to develop new areas of your business and continue growing professionally. Commit to being in the mainstream of your specialization. Join the appropriate professional organizations; receive relevant journals or magazines. Verify that you are on the mailing lists of relevant distributors of products you use. If possible, pursue your own education through workshops or formal schooling, keeping potential new specializations in mind.

Step 6: Growth—Diversification and Expansion

There are four main ways a business can grow:

1. Offering new products and services to existing clients (product development).

2. Offering new products and services to a new population of clients (diversification).

3. Offering your existing products and services to a new population of clients (market development).

4. Improving existing products and services to existing clients (market penetration).

We should approach the expansion of our business through these four methods by constantly improving our products or services, adding to our offerings, targeting new populations, developing new skills in our specializations, or adding a new specialization. Perhaps you make and sell wreaths, so you expand your business by offering classes to teach your skill. A friend of mine is a gourmet cook and she offers educational cooking classes for young children. Perhaps you provide a service that warrants writing articles on the topic. To augment your business, you may want to create an alliance with other women in complimentary specializations to offer workshops or a more complete service or product.

Our growth is only limited by our creativity. A Christian college friend of mine used to say, "I know that I can be creative because I am linked to the Creator."

Step 7: Management

She gets up while it is still dark; she provides food for her family and portions for her servant girls. (Proverbs 31:15)

The godly woman of Proverbs 31 is a capable manager. She knows how to delegate and use her resources. As your specialization grows, you will want to delegate some of your tasks. Perhaps you will want to hire an assistant to train in your specialization and help you. A friend of mine who developed a flower business hired her teenage daughter as her assistant. She is a budding artist and enjoys working with her mom and learning the trade.

Perhaps you will hire some household help. I like to do my own housework because I want my daughters to learn that no one is above physical labor, such as cleaning a toilet. But every four to six weeks I have a cleaning lady come in to help me with the heavy cleaning, which saves me a tremendous amount of time throughout the month. At one time I had a high school girl vacuum my entire house from top to bottom once a month. She helped me and I helped her because she needed the money. You probably have more resources to tap than you realize. Think of your profession on the homefront as a company.

Delegation is actually one aspect of management. Any respected business/management book will tell you that true management is helping people develop to their fullest potential, not "telling them what to do." A manager's job is to remove obstacles so their people can grow. The effective manager is an "enabler," encouraging others to be all that God intends them to be and giving them the tools to do it. The good manager is a servant. The good manager is also a MODEL. He or she leads by example, not by dictatorship. It seems that current business literature has simply discovered the Biblical principles of leadership. Jesus is the finest example we have of an effective manager — from enabling His disciples to go forth to washing their feet at the Last Supper.

These views of management cast a different light on the often misunderstood word *submission*. I am often called "a sweet, little submissive wife" (it is not intended as a compliment!) for three reasons: (1) I am small; (2) I have a quiet, introverted personality; (3) I am married to a "born-leader type" with a very dominant, verbal personality. John is in charge wherever he is. But is this submission?

Submission can be defined as yielding one's way for another. It is doing what is best for another person, not insisting on what is best for us. Are not these the traits of the enabling manager? My husband is the leader of our home, but I am the manager on the homefront. My job is to serve my family and help them become all that God has designed for them to be. I remove any obstacles to their growth. A fine manager cares about people first, his or her clients as well as company employees.

The godly professional woman is also financially responsible and manages money well. She is not in debt. She has enough capital to operate her business and channels incoming funds to improve her services and products.

She does not pursue her specialization *for* the money but she doesn't do it *without* the money. It is a tool not an obsession.

Specialization to Business

I want to share with you my own experiences as an example of "specialization-turned-business." Eight years ago in the midst of my depression over a lost career, a dear friend asked if I would consider giving her daughter piano lessons. "Piano lessons?" I groaned to the Lord. "Was all this preparation to result in being a home piano teacher?" It was the *last* thing that I wanted to do, but it was what God was calling me to do. There was a need and I could fill it. I reluctantly said yes.

I totally enjoyed working with my friend's daughter. I began adding other students, preschoolers through adults. I discovered an innovative music education method that fit ideally with music therapy. I began researching and writing articles on the integration of the two fields. I began taking exceptional students/clients and developed a private practice in music therapy as part of my teaching. Each year I added a new facet to my program. One year I added a group class curriculum to my schedule and the next year I developed a summer creative arts program for young children. Another year I concentrated on my professional writing. Opportunities opened up for the publication of my music. I had one main inspiration for the expansion of my business. I wanted to develop a complete program for my own children. I also kept my student/client load to a minimum in order to not infringe on my time with my family. The professional quality of the program was more important to me than the number of students in it. Business was booming!

I realize now that God was giving me a gift eight years ago. Many people desire to have a business of their own but never have the opportunity to try it. Today I would choose to remain in my own business at home than work for someone else. Professionals on the homefront have the *greater* opportunity. It is interesting to note that in our computer age, men and women of the most sophisticated professions are able to operate out of their homes; it is the wave of the future.

Your specialization can become an effective business (for profit or not) by following these eight steps:

1. Strive for excellence in your specialization.

2. Set a direction and develop a business plan.

3. Develop a professional image.

4. Promote your business effectively.

5. Maintain your high quality business.

6. Diversify and expand.

7. Effectively manage your resources and finances.

8. Care about people first.

Reality Check

Hard work has gotten a bad name. Despite the almost sacred place that workaholism appears to hold in our culture, when it counts most, hard work has a bad reputation. Somewhere along the way we have equated working hard with being miserable. I see this reaction in people's faces when I tell them that my marriage is hard work, being a parent is hard work, a certain friendship is hard work, or my job is hard work. I see them thinking, "I am sorry that it is such hard work . . . that you are so unhappy." Am I working hard? Yes! Am I miserable? No!

Hard work is a God-given privilege to contribute, to be part of a solution—not add to a problem. It is the opposite of giving up when faced with a challenge. And life is one challenge after another. Throughout life I have learned that I receive the greatest gains from the tasks that I work hardest at to master—from learning new skills to jobs, schooling, relationships, and other life tasks. My investment of time and energy has been directly proportional to how valuable and meaningful the gain is. It is the flip side of "Easy come. Easy go." When we work hard toward a goal, the rewards are lasting.

Hard work demands perseverance, which often involves sacrifice, to reach ultimate goals. Hard work is not misery, nor is it our enemy. It is our calling to be faithful to God's purposes. Hard work is our friend.

Time for Reflection

1. Is your specialization a ministry, ministry/business, or for-profit business?

2. Following the above outline, develop a business plan for your specialization.

   Refer to the bibliography and Appendix D for a list of business and marketing resources.

A generous man will prosper; he who refreshes others will himself be refreshed.

(Proverbs 11:25)

PHILANTHROPIC WOMEN

N ow the godly professional woman comes full circle.
She began with caring about people and her final
result is caring about people. She is a philanthropist.

> She opens her arms to the poor and extends her hands to
> the needy. (Proverbs 31:20)

> He who is kind to the poor lends to the LORD, and he
> will reward him for what he has done. (Proverbs 19:17)

Philanthropy can be defined as a love for mankind, as
actively promoting human welfare, and as goodwill toward
one's fellowmen.

The godly woman is concerned for the needy, forgotten people of this world. She seeks them out, realizing that
they are not in her everyday line of vision. She knows that
people are needy, emotionally as well as physically. The
philanthropist donates her resources of time, skills, and
money to help them and mirror Jesus Christ. Philanthropy

is an extension of her specialization and part of her service to the community.

Our philanthropic service should be focused. We cannot heal the hurts of the entire world, but we can target one area. We can support a starving child overseas, help support a mission organization, volunteer our time at a local hospital or support organization, provide transportation for the aging who live in a senior facility, raise funds for the Cancer Society, or meet any number of needs.

One way to seek out your initial areas of philanthropy is to remember how God saved you, what your weaknesses are, or what your family identifies with. Since I became a Christian during college, I give to organizations like Inter-Varsity that minister on secular college campuses. My older daughter tithes her allowance to support another young girl overseas, exactly her age. They exchange letters and pictures. Philanthropy makes for excellent family outreach projects. As a young person, I lost my favorite grandmother to cancer and found it very rewarding to work as a candystriper with the aging in the hospital. What experiences in your past clue you to your specialized area of philanthropy?

Generous Spirit

Philanthropy is also an attitude of generosity. We should be seen as givers *not* takers.

> A gift opens the way for the giver and ushers him into the presence of the great. (Proverbs 18:16)

> Many curry favor with a ruler, and everyone is the friend of a man who gives gifts. (Proverbs 19:6)

God intends for us to be philanthropic in our daily lives as well as in the communities of our world. Gift giving is essential. Do not confuse philanthropy with wealth. It is more a product of time and thoughtfulness than of money. The simplest gifts—a bouquet of flowers from your garden, homemade bread, a certificate for babysitting—can be treasures. Biblical generosity has no price tag. Giving of *ourselves* is the key.

Answer these four questions to examine your generous spirit. It is one thing to yearly give thousands of dollars to a mission organization and another to live it out every day.

1. Do you:

   - give gifts only when it is necessary (birthday, Christmas)?

   - look for every opportunity to give gifts and celebrate individual people?

2. Your reason for calling a friend is more often:

   - to offer to do something nice for them.

   - to ask a favor.

3. Do you:

   - negotiate the minimal amount for services? (One hotel owner said that "Christians" were always the stingiest tippers.)

   - show your gratefulness by paying above the minimum for services? Are you a generous tipper?

4. Do you:

   - tithe your ten percent regularly? Are you a legalist?

● give abundantly whenever you see a need—in or out of your church?

The godly professional woman does not confuse stewardship with stinginess. She is a gift-giver. She gives more time to others than she takes. She is generous with the people around her—from the bellboy at a hotel to a family who has just lost their income. She is a giver not a taker, just as our Lord is. Philanthropy can actually be the professional woman's specialization.

Reality Check

My birthday falls on Christmas, the most hectic day of the year. Only a few special friends used to remember my birthday. Most other friends were too busy. I never expected them to remember because I was as busy as they were!

When I moved to the homefront, I was shocked that first Christmas. *All* my new friends remembered by birthday. They even gave me a surprise one-half birthday party six months later.

They took the time to give of their resources to minister to my needs. These women may not have been giving millions to fund a new medical center—but they were real-life philanthropists.

Time for Reflection

Consider your "generosity quotient." How do you give of your time, talents, and money to your friends, church, community, nation, and world? How can you give more without sacrificing your generosity to your family?

Therefore go and make disciples of all nations. . . .

(Matthew 28:19)

ELEVEN

EVANGELISTS

P hilanthropy is critical because it is the beginning of evangelism. The one calling common to every Christian — man or woman, homefront professional or traveling executive, boy or girl — is to share Jesus Christ with unbelievers. This task is not optional.

Professionals on the homefront have an especially vital evangelistic ministry because they are involved with such a wide range of people — or *should be*. Being home-based is not being home-isolated. Home isolation is a distortion of the Biblical message of dedication on the homefront.

"As you sent me into the world, I have sent them into the world" (John 17:18). We are called to go out into the world. Whenever you are involved with people, you are *out there*. You are out in the world when a neighbor sits at your kitchen table for lunch, you volunteer one morning in your child's classroom, or you share your specialization with someone in the community. We are evangelists, and our chief task is to teach our children to be evangelists.

Training our Children

"Even a child is known by his actions, by whether his conduct is pure and right" (Proverbs 20:11).

We Christian parents are cautious today for good reason. In our wicked world, we fear that our children will be abducted, abused, molested, given drugs and alcohol, shown pornography, sexually used, taught unbiblical principles, drawn into a cult or the occult, and exposed to numerous other horrors. We long to protect our children from an evil world. Being a cautious, fearful person by nature, I would like to lock the doors and keep my children safe forever. Yes, I am "overprotective" of these treasures of God. My behavior is loving, but this is the question I've had to face: Is it Biblical?

Well-meaning families send their children to Christian schools, home school them, keep them out of secular activities in the community by offering similar ones in the church (church baseball teams, Pioneer girls, etc.) — all in a loving effort to protect them from evil influences. The same families who financially support Inter-Varsity and Campus Crusade on secular campuses send their children to Christian colleges. The same families who provide a one-week Vacation Bible School to reach the community refuse to send their children to public school. We give our money and time, but we will not give what is most precious to us — our children, our first fruits.

People reassure, "It's a wonderful program. Our children have only Christian influences." But who is the child influencing? And who is the parent influencing? Scripture is very clear on this point: Our mission is to go out into the world and share the love of Jesus Christ with unbelievers. The parents' job is to train children for this mission. God sets no age requirements for serving Him. There was another group who was obsessed with not being contaminated with the evil world. They were Pharisees. We know how Jesus felt about them! And we know how they felt about Jesus associating with unbelievers!

As much as I would like to escape the Biblical fact that my children are called into the world as I am, there is one reason I cannot. God never lets me forget that I was once that unsaved little girl in grade school, that unbelieving student in high school, and that confused college student on a secular campus. I know that I would not be a Christian today if it were not for the Christian children in my grade school who shared Jesus on the playground, high school friends who took me to church with them, and the student Bible study leaders on my college campus. Each influence played a critical part in my salvation.

Young people are best evangelized by other young people. Peer evangelism is an established fact in foreign missionary programs, evidenced by the focus on training native populations to evangelize their own people. Learning to share Jesus with others is a process, a skill to be developed. It cannot be learned in a vacuum. A basic fact of all good education is that children most easily learn what is useful to them in their everyday world. Skills must be applied to real life. It is one thing to memorize Scripture for hours and another to know what to do with it on the battlefield.

Imagine the concert pianist, who practices for years for his debut at Carnegie Hall, forgetting to sell tickets. He ends up playing to an empty hall. Sometimes we become so obsessed with preparation that we lose sight of the greater purpose.

Our faith is not an isolationist belief. This is no time for present-day monasteries. Monks separated themselves from the people; they did not reach them.

Biblical Common Sense

This plea for battling the enemy must be balanced with Biblical common sense. No one sends untrained soldiers into a battle unprepared. Each child matures at different rates. Parents will know when their child is ready to wisely and *gradually* enter the battle. Going into the world is not sending a two-year-old to a day-care center or encouraging your teenager to hang out with drug addicts, alcoholics, or the sexually promiscuous. God issues very strict warnings about not surrounding ourselves with bad company, because He knows that we will drown. Our anchor is fellow Christians.

I am also not suggesting that we close all Christian schools, abandon home schooling, and terminate church programs. Some of them can be used as excellent outreaches to the community. As a teacher, I see great value in these programs and am personally involved in some of them. But then we have a responsibility to provide other evangelism opportunities for these young soldiers through spending time with neighborhood friends or unsaved extended family, volunteering at a hospital, or taking the church musical to Juvenile Hall, for example.

Our evil world today is no different than the evil world of New Testament times. Torture, sexual perversion, cults, and self-worship abounded. It was *not* a safe place. The evil one never changes. He was just as scary and powerful then as he is today.

The less salt and light of Jesus Christ in the world, the more evil runs rampant. When we Christians pull out of the mainstream of life, we give Satan free reign. He applauds us. By our absence, we actually make the world a *more* evil place. Evil is the enemy, not the people captured by him.

Evangelism Models

The way we train young evangelists is by *modeling* the process for them. We go before our children to lead them, just as Jesus Christ goes before us.

If you send your child to public school, you share the ministry by volunteering in the classroom, acting as room mother, encouraging your child's friends to come over to play, praying for them, becoming involved with other school mothers, having the teacher for dinner, or driving school friends to church programs and summer Vacation Bible School. If your child is involved in community activities, become a Girl Scout leader or baseball coach. Get involved with your neighbors and have each family over for dinner through the year. Choose an outreach and be committed as a family. Effective evangelism is rooted in lovingly cultivated relationships.

Real-Life Lessons

My first grade daughter, Janelle, came home very upset from school yesterday. Her favorite time, recess, was being ruined by an older child named Kristine. Kristine was bullying the first graders on the playground, making fun of them, calling them names, and generally making their lives miserable.

My first human response was indignation. My child should not be subjected to that kind of treatment! Then God showed me the blatant hypocrisy. This lesson was exactly why we had purposefully decided to send our children to public school in our community. This was only the beginning. And I was reacting to this?

Janelle and I talked about how much love Kristine needed — how much she needed Jesus. Janelle was God's light. We covenanted to pray for Kristine nightly. We also discussed how important it was for Janelle to never forget how it felt to be bullied. As long as she kept that in mind, she wouldn't do it to someone else and could stand up to protect others.

The first night, Janelle said, "Well, you can pray for Kristine if you want . . . but *I'm not*! I don't like her. She's all black and ugly inside." "Black and ugly inside . . . just like us without Jesus," I explained. "Liking someone has nothing to do with loving someone. God's love is loving someone no matter what — loving them when we can't like them. That's our job." Janelle was beginning to understand. We now pray for Kristine nightly. She has become our love project. I am convinced that my children's most important spiritual lessons will not be learned in Sunday school or our daily Bible time (those are preparation times), but on the "playground of life."

Reality Check

Do you view unsaved, disobedient little hellions as bad influences on your children? Or do you see them as children who need the love of Jesus Christ and your children as God's tools to reach them?

Worse yet, do your children have trouble tolerating other children who have different lifestyles and values? Or do they understand that God's unconditional love starts with unlovable people — sinners just like them?

God's foreign missionaries of tomorrow start with the young neighborhood evangelists of today.

Remember "Ships are safe in the harbor, but that's not what ships are for."

Be strong and courageous. Do not be afraid or terrified because of them, for the Lord your God goes with you; he will never leave you nor forsake you. (Deuteronomy 31:6)

Time for Reflection

1. Who are you sharing Jesus Christ with? How are you "out in the world"?

2. How are you training your children to evangelize? What are their opportunities?

3. How are you modeling evangelism for your children?

Therefore, my dear brothers, stand firm.
Let nothing move you. Always give your-
selves fully to the work of the Lord, because you know that your labor in the
Lord is not in vain.

(1 Corinthians 15:58)

TWELVE

THE KEY: PERSEVERANCE

B ecoming a godly professional woman on the homefront is a challenging, difficult task. The key to pursuing this goal can be summed up in one Biblical word:
perseverance. Perseverance is hanging tough in the face of
insurmountable obstacles. It is holding on to Jesus Christ
and His vision for you when everyone says you are a failure. Perseverance is not giving up when the world looks
black, God seems absent, and your overwhelming loneliness even drives you to thoughts of suicide. Perseverance
is survival.

It is a Biblical fact that if you seek to follow God
wholeheartedly, you will meet with opposition. The Bible
is filled with stories of people who paid the price for remaining steadfast to God. The Scriptures call it persecution; our world calls it rejection. To be cast off is not an
experience unique only to Christians.

Did you know that:

- William Faulkner dropped out of college and flunked his English course?

- The first audience to hear Stravinsky's *Rite of Spring*, the most significant music work of our century, was so offended that they broke out in a riot?

- Lucille Ball dropped out of high school and was repeatedly told that she had no talent?

- E. B. White's book, *Stuart Little*, met with rejection for seven years. The children's librarian emeritus of the New York Public Library wrote that the book would be damaging to children and the project should be abandoned immediately.

Albert Einstein said, "Great spirits have always encountered violent opposition from mediocre minds." Even the greats, perhaps especially the greats, experience rejection. No wonder our Lord Jesus Christ was murdered on a cross. Those who follow Him will also endure persecution.

Victim Theology

Be wary of a dangerous, subtle message pervading some churches today. I firmly believe in God's control. He knows what He is doing with my life, and I trust Him fully. Yet sometimes this theology is twisted by the enemy. It is perverted to "victim theology." Whenever you hit an obstacle or a brick wall, friends may say, "Do you think God is trying to tell you something?" The message is that if life gets tough, you must be on the wrong track. Give up! Are we victims of our circumstances? No! We are victorious soldiers fighting a battle. We are on the winning side. This world is our training ground. We are called to persevere for God's purposes.

The Brick Wall

I have hit brick walls many times in my life, and God has miraculously plowed through each one. One of the most dramatic incidences occurred when I was out of college looking for work. I had worked part-time, but now John and I needed a full-time second income in order to buy a home. Therapy jobs were few and far between, and I had exhausted all my resources. "Okay, Lord, I give up," I said.

My parents had always encouraged me to take business secretarial courses and work during summers. They supported my goals and vision but wanted me to have back-up skills to make a living when necessary. That time had come.

I saw all my dreams going up in smoke as I drove to the secretarial placement service. The interviewer read my resume and said, "You don't want this job, do you?" "Not really," I sighed. The interviewer responded, "Well, off the record, I used to work at the children's hospital. I know the director of the therapy program there. Go see her and tell her I sent you. No charge." "Now?" I asked. "Right now!" she said.

Totally out of character, I got up my nerve and drove there immediately. I later learned that the director never saw anyone without an appointment. She spoke with me, explaining that one of the therapists had quit *the day before*. A week later I had the job. God had parted the Red Sea.

Continually I am amazed at God's miraculous leading in my life. If there are no brick walls, He can't plow through them. If there are no obstacles, we will never learn perseverance. Remember that the most critical time to hang tough is when you are most tempted to give up.

Persevering Strength

Perseverance is defined as persisting, remaining steadfast, in a task in spite of counter influences, opposition, and discouragement. Our enemy hates perseverance! His goal is to cause us to despair and quit.

Persecution is defined as harassment in a manner to injure, grieve, afflict, and cause to suffer. Who or what persecutes you? Is it your circumstances? your neighbors? some "well-meaning" friends? your husband? your children? your community? Who tempts you to drop out of battle?

God calls us to be strong, steadfast women. What is your picture of a "strong woman"? Perhaps it is a strong personality or a charismatic leader. Maybe it is an independent woman. Perhaps it is someone who doesn't back down to anyone or is not easily intimidated. Maybe it is someone who can control a situation or impose her will on others.

Stereotypes abound concerning the strong woman in our culture. Some of the above qualities are even admirable but are they consistent with Biblical strength? Remember that the woman of Proverbs 31 was "clothed with strength and dignity" (vs. 25a). <u>True strength is defined as the capacity for endurance and the power to resist force and attack.</u> Biblical strength is perseverance, the ability to stand firm against temptation. It is going God's way instead of our own way. Ironically this tougher path is often viewed as weakness in our culture. Biblical strength is strength in the Lord. It is not retaliating when you have been wronged. It is depending fully on God and obeying Him. It is loving others unconditionally no matter how they treat you and putting others' needs before your own. It is sacrificing for the cause of Christ and mirroring God's love in a hurting world.

One of my favorite children's stories is the fable of the wind and the sun. I offer it as an example of Biblical strengths versus worldly strength:

One day the Wind and the Sun began to argue. "I am the strongest," said the Wind. "No, I am the strongest," said the Sun. This argument went on and on until they decided to put the matter to a test.

"Look at the man walking down the road," said the Sun. "Let us see which of us can throw off his cape." "It is no contest. I will easily win," said the Wind. And he began to blow and blow. The harder he blew, the colder it grew. And the colder it grew, the more the man would hug the cape around himself. At last the Wind gave up.

The Sun smiled and began to grow warmer and warmer. The man stopped hugging the cape around himself and let it flap about his shoulders. Then, as the Sun grew warmer and warmer, the man threw it off altogether.

The Sun had won with gentleness what the Wind could not win with force.

Are you persecuted and rejected? Kill them with kindness! It is much more powerful.

Persevering Guides

If one falls down, his friend can help him up. But pity
to the man who falls and has no one to help him up!
(Ecclesiastes 4:10)

We are not meant to persevere alone. God goes before
us to lead us and sends people to encourage us along the
way. I guarantee you that no one has the ideal life. We each
have our own unique set of hurts and discouragements.

Resist him, standing firm in the faith, because you know
that your brothers throughout the world are undergoing
the same kind of sufferings. (1 Peter 5:9)

We all endure suffering. No one is exempt. Our calling
is to become persevering guides for each other, our husbands, children, friends, extended family, stretching to
missionaries on the most distant shore. We come alongside
to say, "Don't give up. I'll go through this with you." We
encourage others to persevere in three ways:

1. *Catch the vision* that God has given them—whether you
   agree with it or not. We each know what it feels like to
   share our vision and dreams with someone, who in turn
   lovingly "rains all over our parade" with a brutal dose of
   reality and practicality. Usually these people have no
   dreams of their own. *Listen* to people share their vision
   of God's purpose for their lives.

2. *Encourage others with affirming words* and gestures of
   thoughtfulness and support. Make a phone call, send a
   card, take a gift, invite out for coffee—communicate that
   you love this person unconditionally and he or she is
   special to you.

3. *Take action* or "put your money where your mouth is."
Be willing to do actual tasks. Find out what is overwhelming the person right now and offer practical help.
Is a new mother up with her baby all night? Take the
family dinner and do their wash. Are your friends having marriage problems? Take their children for the
weekend so they can get away together. Is a friend
struggling with severe depression? Drive her to her
counseling appointments.

Some of us are more adept at offering comforting
words. Others are expert at springing into action. Our Biblical goal is to do *both*, as our Lord does. But realistically
we will be stronger at one than the other. God will use us
for His purposes.

I have had the privilege of having exceptional, persevering guides in my life. There have been friends who
knew just the right thing to say to encourage me. I have
been blessed with my parents and husband who are people
of action. They know just the thing to do to accomplish a
greater purpose.

I am more comfortable offering affirming words. My
eldest daughter, cut from her father's mold, usually ends
up saying, "Mom, that's enough of that lovey-mushy
stuff . . . what are we going to *do* about this? I want
Daddy now." It is important to know what will be most
helpful at the right time.

Keep your eyes open for people who need persevering
guides. People ready to give up usually do not ask for
help. You will only be able to encourage them if you
know perseverance firsthand in your own life. "[Love] always protects, always trusts, always hopes, always perse-
veres. Love never fails" (1 Corinthians 13:7–8a).

Reality Check

I was sitting alone in a hotel room late at night, crying and overwhelmed. It was a dark time in our lives. Illness, excessive pressures, and marital struggles closed in on us. I cried out to the Lord for comfort. God, the ultimate persevering guide, came to me in a very real way — and not the way I expected or desired. There were no embracing arms. He looked me straight in the eye and said: "Have I asked you to be imprisoned for my sake?"

"No, Lord."

"Have I asked you to die for my sake?"

"No, Lord."

"Have I asked you to be blind, deaf, or crippled?"

"No, Lord."

"Have I asked you to be homeless and starve?"

"No, Lord."

The questions went on and then: "All I have asked is that you love this husband, be a mother, suffer some illness, do these other tasks I've given you . . . and you *can't even do this?*"

Yes, God was calling me a wimp! It was tough love and it was life-changing. God's children are not wimps. Relying completely on His strength, we will persevere.

Time for Reflection

1. In what areas do you struggle with perseverance?

2. Do you view yourself as a Biblically strong woman? or a victim?

3. How can you become a persevering guide? Are you better at:

a. catching the vision?
b. affirming with words?
c. encouraging with actions?

What do you need to work on? List some people who need your encouraging guidance, starting with your own family.

You will keep him in perfect peace, whose mind is stayed on You, because he trusts in You.

(Isaiah 26:3, NKJV)

AVOIDING THE STRESSAHOLIC SYNDROME

I have saved the most important part of our journey together until last to leave you with perspective. There is a fine line between being an industrious professional woman and being a *stressaholic*—someone who is addicted to stress. This woman cannot stop! She has to be constantly productive and pushes herself far beyond what any human being should be expected to accomplish. Stress, defined as tension resulting from factors which alter our normal equilibrium, is healthy in moderation. It is the normal response of our bodies to demands and pressures. This is good stress: eustress. But excessive, prolonged stress can have disastrous results on us and those around us. This is bad stress: distress.

Our body's main response to stress is to produce adrenalin. Dr. Hart points out in his excellent book, *Adrenalin and Stress,* that people who fill their lives with constant stress are actually "adrenalin addicts." They can't relax. They can't sleep well at night. Their body system never returns to a normal state. Like any addiction, stress addicts fall into the vicious cycle of seeking out more stress. They are hooked on that high level of adrenalin in their systems.

I know about the Stressaholic Syndrome because I am a recovering stressaholic and I am married to a stressaholic.

Stressaholic Patterns

There are two main types of stressaholics. I am "a developed stress addict." Since my parents were very dedicated workers and not followers of Christ, I learned at a young age that my worth was based in my accomplishments. They felt that whatever I did, it could be better because it could be *perfect*. In first grade I brought home my first homework assignment to write the alphabet. My mother worked on it with me until it was perfect. The next day the teacher displayed it on the board as the best one in the class. The classic Stressaholic Syndrome was born. A couple months later, to my horror, I was promoted to second grade. I was then the youngest and the smallest child in the class and felt twice the pressure to succeed. I didn't feel that it was optional to not be the best. Perfectionism, overachievement, and stress addiction often go hand in hand. I believed that if I could just work hard enough, then I could be rewarded. Yearly the syndrome became more intense until I went away to a prestigious college. I was shocked to receive my first *C*. When I talked to the professor, he said, "You don't understand. To get a *C* is doing very well here. You *are* average. Every student here is a former parliamentarian, winner of this award or that award." None of us were "the best" anymore, and it was the best thing that could happen to any of us.

Like many of my classmates, a deep depression accompanied my realization that I could no longer accomplish my way to worthiness. A friend then took me to a campus Bible study, and I received Jesus Christ in a very real and exciting way. God loved me *unconditionally*. Jesus had accomplished it all for me on the cross. I was free from my prison of achieving worth. God accepted me, loved me, and rescued me the way that I was.

But slowly and insidiously the old patterns crept back in, and I began applying them to my life of faith. There were Bible study times to structure and ministries to be involved in! One of my professors in graduate school even wrote on one of my research papers, "This is very good work, but I think that you should take some time out to smell the flowers."

I was a driven person. My body kept signaling me that this was not my natural bent. Because I am a private introvert, all my drive was turned inward. I preferred to work alone. And I suffered from becoming sick often. I ran my body to a point where it was susceptible to every illness. The patterns were dangerous.

My husband is a very different type of stressaholic. It is his natural bent to thrive on constant activity, challenge, and pressure. He came out of the womb that way! His mother deserves a medal of honor for having survived raising him.

At a very young age his parents had to put netting over his crib to keep him from crawling out of it all through the night. He was in and out of emergency rooms as a child due to his "creative methods."

John's father was project director for the *Explorer I* project. John was one-and-one-half years old during their trip to Cape Canaveral. Exhausted from the trip, the family went to sleep. John's mom woke up at 3 A.M. to see her son running along the beach. He had gotten out of the crib, opened the hotel room door, and was having a great time! John has not stopped moving from his infancy to this present day. Because he is an extrovert and born leader, he is driven to constant activity with groups of people. He is not simply a workaholic because his addiction to constant pressure permeates his church life and hobbies as well. When he discovers a new hobby, he is completely obsessed with it until he masters it. He is happily driven.

Changing Stressaholic Patterns

For many years of our marriage I tried to keep up with my husband's constant activity. My old stressaholic patterns had prepared me well for this fast-paced life. But I always knew one thing: the stressaholic life was no way to raise children. Bill Butterworth, one of my favorite speakers, says it perfectly: "Children are slow-poke people in a hurry-up world."

When I became pregnant with our first child, I realized that it was time to end the life of constant stress. I didn't want to pass the syndrome on to my children. My husband could not change, but I could.

The godly professional woman of Scripture is *not* a stressaholic. She is balanced. She puts relationships first. She has time for those around her, especially her family. She employs her organizational skills and specialization to create more time in her day. She takes care of herself physically. She is not driven; she rests in God.

If you struggle with the Stressaholic Syndrome, I can offer you concrete ways to fight it which have helped me.

Retreat Times

Plan retreat breaks in your day, week, month, and year. God had a retreat of rest after His work on Creation. He commands us to do the same through the Sabbath. Unfortunately, the Sabbath is often the busiest day of the week for us. Between ministries in the morning service, having people for dinner after church, and returning for activities in the evening service, Sunday is my most stressful day! The solution is to plan other retreat times. Plan a break in your day to treat yourself. Make your retreat time with God a priority. Have your Bible study over your favorite snack. Read a good book or take a short nap. Put your feet up and look at your favorite magazine. Go out for coffee with a friend. Take just one-half hour for refreshment and don't let "productivity" creep into that time. Plan similar breaks in your children's days. Plan a quiet, unstructured day in your week or at least in your month. We call these "Snuggle Days" at our house. We don't *plan* anything and just let the day happen. My children ask, "What are we doing today?" and I say, "Anything we want."

Plan a retreat week during the year. Perhaps it is your family vacation or a week on the homefront that you block our for your "mental health." Put your break times on the calendar. (If I don't plan them, I don't take them.)

My husband's family owns a home in Idaho. We commit to retreat there twice a year, once in the winter and once in the summer. It is a complete break from work, church, and home pressures. Our retreat time is not simply a family vacation — it is our survival measure!

After completing a major project, make yourself take a day off. Most stressaholics are high achievers. People marvel at how much they get accomplished. Stress addicts usually have a list of projects to do a mile long. They live with the delusion that if they can push to finish this one project, then they can relax. But they continually jump into the next project without a break. They create for themselves an underlying anxiety that time is running out. Stressaholics must force themselves to take a break after a period of concentrated work.

Traditions

In addition to unstructured retreat times, plan family traditions as a priority. Look for every opportunity to create a celebration. Holidays are obvious times for special celebrations, but more important are those times of tradition which are unique just to your family. I have enjoyed researching traditions with our children. We developed a tradition calendar for the year which has grown to include one celebration a week. Sometimes we celebrate a famous composer's birthday complete with birthday cake and his music. Authors are fun to celebrate. On A. A. Milne's birthday (the author of *Winnie the Pooh*) we have a "Bear Party" and fix dishes prepared with honey. On the date of each of our children's birthdays during the month, we make that their "Special Day." We go pumpkin picking in October and have a Pumpkin Party. We include foreign customs in honor of our different heritages. We continually add new discoveries to our tradition calendar. The possibilities are endless if you simply focus on the celebration of being a family. Look for every excuse for a mini-party!

Traditions are important for any family, but they are doubly important for stressaholic parents. Traditions make you stop whatever work you are involved in to celebrate and focus on each other. Commit to celebrating any tradition on its specified day with no option to change it, just as you wouldn't celebrate Christmas or your birthday the day after. You are building family retreat times into your life to occur year after year.

My husband, children, and I have the privilege of being a "transitional tradition family." We are the first of our respective generations to become followers of Jesus Christ, and we are the first to create our own set of traditions. I envy people who say, "We've had this tradition in our family for 100 years." It is our hope that our grandchildren's grandchildren will say that about the traditions that we set today.

Accepting Imperfection

The third step in avoiding becoming a stressaholic is to be content with imperfection. Accept that life will never be perfect. When stressaholics work toward perfection in their tasks, they are saying by their actions that Christ died in vain. God sent our precious Lord Jesus to die for imperfect sinners.

It is one thing to do a fine job to the glory of God and another to be driven by perfectionism. I have encouraged my children to focus on the good that they do, not on their mistakes. Being aware of our mistakes is different from focusing on them.

Accept that certain times in your life are *not* going to be productive in terms of accomplishment. Transition times of major change, such as a move, pregnancy, the birth of a new baby, the loss of a loved one, or a job change for your husband require survival measures. Do not expect any more of yourself than to simply adjust to the change.

Accepting the Stressaholic Spouse

A common phenomenon in our culture occurs when the stressaholic wife decides to slow down to raise the children and the stressaholic husband is at a point in his career where he doubles his activity rate. I have experienced this situation firsthand, and it is a tough battle. If you are in a similar battle, I offer you "Survival Guidelines for Living with the Overstressed Spouse".

1. You must be committed 100 percent to the relationship (50/50 may be fair but it's not Biblical).

2. You cannot change your spouse. Do not add to his pressures by trying. Accept him unconditionally.

3. Do not spend what little time you have together arguing about the time you don't have with him.

4. Plan family tradition times that he won't want to miss. If he can't come home, take the party to him. For example, take a picnic to his office or meet him for dinner.

5. Eliminate chores and other stresses around the house for him so that he can spend time at home with the children.

6. Consistently remind your children of their good memories of their dad when he is out of town or working late at night. Communicate to them how much he loves them. Keep him part of the family when he's absent. Expressing your frustrations to your children will only hurt your children.

7. To fight your loneliness, develop an informal support group of wives in the same situation. Meet for dinner with your children.

8. Communicate openly (not critically) about your feelings. Being the "silent martyr" can make for peace on the homefront, but it has disastrous results on a relationship.

9. Continue your relationship by sending your husband cards or other surprises. Initiate planning times to spend as a couple. Work at being part of his life despite his schedule.

10. Develop your own professional specialization to constructively fill up lonely hours and not depend on or pressure your husband to meet *all* your human self-esteem needs.

11. Be involved in your husband's activities when possible, but do not fall into the same stressaholic patterns. Encourage his interests which can include the whole family.

Sometimes I am asked how I continue to teach and write with small children at home. The answer is simple: No one has the ideal life. My husband's job has always required him to work long hours into the late evening. (Often he comes home for dinner, or we meet at a restaurant, before he returns to work. He makes spending special time with our children an absolute priority.) So I have a choice. I can sit at home at night feeling sorry for myself

and thinking things I shouldn't, *or* I can fill up the time
with constructive purposes. Destructive or constructive
time — it is my choice.

You can survive living with a stressaholic spouse, but
it is hard work. More important, I hope that I have shown
that *you* don't want to be the stressaholic member of your
family. You can fight this syndrome by:

- Planning personal retreat times.

- Making your time with God a priority.

- Planning family retreat times (traditions).

- Accepting imperfection in your life.

- Accepting and supporting a stressaholic spouse while not
  falling into his patterns. One parent must be the anchor.

Verses for the Stressaholic

Unless the Lord builds the house, its builders labor in
vain. Unless the Lord watches over the city, the watch-
men stand guard in vain. In vain you rise early and stay
up late, toiling for food to eat — for he grants sleep to
those he loves. (Psalm 127:1–2)

My heart is not proud, O Lord, my eyes are not
haughty; I do not concern myself with great matters or
things too wonderful for me. But I have stilled and qui-
eted my soul; like a weaned child with its mother, like a
weaned child is my soul within me. O Israel, put your
hope in the Lord both now and forevermore. (Psalm
131:1–3)

Reality Check

We stressaholics must discipline ourselves to take "holidays" daily, weekly, monthly, and yearly. A holiday is defined as a period of relaxation and celebration; a vacation; a time exempt from work. It comes from the word *holy day,* a day set apart to the service of God. No wonder we derive the word *sabbatical* from the Sabbath.

Here we can learn a lesson from the secular working world. Professional women take year-long sabbaticals to avoid burnout and six-month maternity leaves to focus on their families. Professionals on the homefront should not be denied the same privileges. I am not suggesting that you *abandon* your family (your "work") for a year any more than secular professionals do. But you can take six-month and one-year breaks from certain activities, businesses, or specializations, and you will return more refreshed the next year. I make it a practice to take a maternity leave from church activities and my business with each new child.

We as home professionals must encourage each other to take breaks and give each other the freedom to forego activities for one year without pressure. We must fight the stressaholic burnout syndrome together.

Time for Reflection

1. Do you fall into stressaholic patterns? If so, how will you fight this syndrome?

2. Are you married to a stressaholic spouse? If so, how will you creatively survive your situation and support your husband?

3. Are you producing stressaholic children? How can you avoid this?

Refer to the bibliography and Appendix D for resources on stress and family traditions. You will find a Family Traditions: Idea Checklist in Appendix C.

You are the light of the world. A city on a hill cannot be hidden. Neither do people light a lamp and put it under a bowl. Instead they put it on its stand, and it gives light to everyone in the house. In the same way, let your light shine before men, that they may see your good deeds and praise your Father in heaven.

(Matthew 5:14–16)

For this very reason, make every effort to add to your faith goodness; and to goodness, knowledge; and to knowledge, self-control; and to self-control, perseverance; and to perseverance, godliness; and to godliness, brotherly kindness; and to brotherly kindness, love. For if you possess these qualities in increasing measure, they will keep you from being ineffective and unproductive in your knowledge of our Lord Jesus Christ.

(2 Peter 1:5–8)

CONCLUSION

O ne of my favorite children's stories is *The Country Bunny and the Little Gold Shoes,* written by DuBose Hayward (Houghton Mifflin Co., 1939). It is a wonderful celebration of industrious women, complete with spiritual analogies. As a young bunny, the heroine longs to deliver Easter eggs to needy girls and boys. Upon becoming a mother to twenty-one babies and being laughed at by the other bunnies for her vision, she slowly gives up her dream. She works hard to create a loving home and passes on a different specialization to each of her children as they grow up. Her home is the most well-managed one in town, and still the other bunnies laugh.

When the Great Grandfather Bunny comes to pick one special bunny to deliver eggs for him that year, he chooses our Mother Bunny for her great compassion and the many skills she evidences in her home. He enables her to go on the most difficult journey of all, to take an Easter egg to a sick little boy living on the highest mountain. Her family shares her vision and love for Great Grandfather Bunny.

The Country Bunny is a special traditional story that we read every Easter in our home, but it is also a beautiful picture of the godly professional woman serving God on the homefront that we can pass on to our children.

May we take hold of this wonderful opportunity and gift of life to teach our children that godly women are:

- focused on God and family first.

- industrious.

- specialized.

- well-organized and prepared.

- capable businesswomen and managers.

- dignified and respected.

- generous and defenders of the needy.

- committed to evangelism.

- strong and persevering.

We are called to be professionals and are rewarded accordingly:

Giver her the reward she has earned, and let her works bring her praise at the city gate. (Proverbs 31:31)

Final Reality Check

We had a couple over for dinner last night. They have no children; the wife is a well-educated executive businesswoman who commutes daily to a major city an hour away.

As I was busy preparing dinner in the kitchen, my tired, hungry, cranky children hugged my legs at the end of a long day. The bewildered look on the wife's face told me that she wasn't quite sure how to approach me. As the evening progressed, I had to rise from the dinner table several times to perform "mother duties" (from pouring extra glasses of milk to cleaning up spills to putting pajamas on and telling bedtime stories). I noticed that she was conversing comfortably with my executive husband and her husband, but she had no idea what to talk about with me. "What could we possibly have in common?" her eyes told me. I tried to ask her questions about her work, but she would change the topic to "homemaking questions" about dinner and wallpaper. She apparently thought that those were safe topics that interested me or I could handle. I started to wonder if I should have put myself to bed with the kids! I then flashed back to my former life where my colleagues thought that "ignorance" was synonymous with "being at home." I had to smile. God had certainly brought me full-circle in my transition to being a professional on the homefront. He had performed a miracle in remolding me—my thoughts, direction, and purpose. I felt no compunction to explain my journey or defend my lifestyle. It was a gift from my Heavenly Father. I felt very loved by Him and simply desired to pour that love into the lives of others. I had "come home" in more ways than one.

Time for Reflection

Summarize your personal professional calling from God.

TASK LISTS

(To be augmented with your individual tasks)

Daily

- Bible study
- Exercise
- Meal preparation
- Straightening house
- Family activity time (individual time with each child)

Weekly

- Plan week
- Menu planning
- Market
- Errands (cleaners, library, bank, etc.)
- Paper work (correspondence)
- Laundry (linens, wash brushes)
- Housecleaning
- Yard work
- Water inside plants
- Hospitality
- Project Day: Home/family projects
- Specialization projects

- Volunteer work (in community, at child's school)
- Children's activities

Bi-Weekly

- Grooming needs — nails, facial, etc.

Monthly

- Planning
- Filing
- Gift shopping for month, catalog orders
- Bill paying, bank statements
- Put month's pictures in album
- Decorating, tradition planning for month
- Mending, clean shoes, etc.
- Possible cooking day (freezing)
- Sort magazines, journals, recipes, etc.
- Get haircut
- Special projects: Home/family

Seasonal — every six months

- Planning: Goal setting
- Spring cleaning, house organization, stocking up on supplies
- Review wardrobe needs, purchase or make (for family also)
- Yard clean-up, planting
- Retreat/Sabbatical Time
- Christmas gift planning (during summer)
- Have children's pictures taken
- Plan special traditions, trips
- Major projects: Home/family

APPENDIX B

PRINCIPLES OF ART AND DESIGN

The following principles will help you in approaching any artistic task, from creating an environment to coordinating an outfit. Interior design is a complex field, with professional training required, but you will find that many of the basic principles are good common sense.

Principles of Design

1. The design must be functional — appropriate to the activity. You wouldn't wear a silk party dress to your son's football game or carpet the high-traffic family room white!

2. The design should be consistent in mood and harmonious in form. This includes a consistent color scheme, proportional pieces (in scale), coordinated styles and textures, and similar quality of pieces. Very expensive and very cheap pieces do not mix. The key is harmony. Being unique and interesting is different from sticking out like a sore thumb. One can be the focal point of the room; the

other doesn't fit. The design of the whole picture must "work."

3. Contrast and variety add interest, yet balance and symmetry should be retained throughout the design: a balance of color, heights, weights, shapes, textures, etc. For example, if your color scheme is blue/green, you wouldn't put all green pieces on one side of the axis of the room and all blue on the other. You wouldn't put all tall pieces on one side and small pieces on the other. You would artistically mix them.

4. The design should have a focal point, a focus. Beautiful architectural features are natural focal points in a room — a lovely fireplace, a bay window with a scenic view. Emphasize that strength and design the room around it. Similarly, choose the most important piece in a room first and build the other pieces around it. Functionally, the most important piece in the bedroom is the bed; in the dining room, the dining table, and so on. A good-looking outfit has one main interesting piece of clothing with matching accessories.

But many of us do not live in architecturally novel houses, but in suburban tract homes. I term these rooms "white boxes." You must then create a focal point — a wall of bookshelves, a unique piece of antique furniture, a huge vase of colorful flowers, or a beautiful picture. The best place for a focal point is the impact wall(s), the wall(s) that you first see when you enter the room.

5. The key to good design is emphasizing the positive and eliminating or camouflaging the negative. If you cannot eliminate a negative, you can at least hide it by blending it into its surroundings.

The positive is not always the "perfect." It can be the unique and different. Our human bodies are excellent examples. No one has the perfect body! We can hide our differences or accentuate them. A very small person can dress to look larger or she can wear tight belts and contrasting colors to emphasize her petiteness.

Similarly you can paint out an unusual feature, such as a column or beam, in a room or use a contrasting color to highlight it. (To "paint out" is to blend into the room with the same color paint or wallpaper.) Ugly, metal windows are a common negative feature. You could eliminate such a window by replacing it with a beautiful wood French door, which would become a focal point. Or you could camouflage it by treating it with shutters.

6. There is nothing essentially wrong with a very large room or a very small room. Some people enjoy big, open airy spaces; others enjoy cozy places. But if you want to change your space, or the perception of your own height, the following techniques will help you.

To make a large room appear smaller:

- Use large pieces. Big rooms need large pieces of furniture.
- Use bold and large patterns.
- Emphasize diversity. Break the room into components. Use contrasting (yet coordinated) trims.
- Dark and warm colors advance. Dark rooms appear smaller and dark walls come closer. Large people wear dark colors to appear thinner.

To make a small room appear larger:

- Use small pieces and patterns.

- Employ light, solid, muted colors. Light and cool colors recede, making walls look larger and father away.

- Emphasize unity. Don't break up the room or have too many details. For example, wall and window treatments should match, not contrast.

- Mirrors can be used effectively to create the illusion of more space.

Vertical lines make things look taller. Horizontal lines shorten. To make a ceiling appear higher, use vertical lines and solids. Don't break up the wall. The ceiling should be painted a light color. To make a ceiling appear shorter, a room cozier, create horizontal lines with wainscoting, chair rails, crown moldings, borders, contrasting paint and wallpaper with the chair rail between. A dark ceiling will come toward you.

7. In trying to create interest and diversity, do not make the error of interrupting the flow of a room. For example, a wall treatment must be consistent. Do not wallpaper half the room and paint the other. This is a common problem in our combination living/dining rooms where the owner tries to define a separate dining room. This approach chops up the room.

Especially in small areas, the wall treatments should be the same on all walls. The window treatments and flooring should remain consistent. Keeping the flow is critical. Be careful to not mix multiple patterns. Usually one main pattern per room suffices.

Also beware of mixing different furniture period styles from different countries. You can sometimes mix different periods from one country or the same period from different countries, but not both!

8. Shapes should be harmonious to space. For example, a vertical wall space needs a vertical wall hanging. If you don't have such a piece, you can create the effect with a collection of smaller hangings that together create that vertical picture. A round alcove requires a similar piece, not a huge rectangular desk.

9. Pieces can appear heavier or lighter depending on the colors and fabrics used. You can add weight with bright colors and bold patterns. You reduce weight with solid or muted colors and simple patterns.

So if you have furniture that is out of proportion, such as a huge couch and a tiny chair, you can (a) make the couch "lighter" with a muted color and (b) make the chair "heavier" with a bright pattern.

Principles of Color

Color is the most powerful tool in design. You can change a mood with color. You can change the perceived temperature of a room with color. You can look bright and cheerful in clothes that suit your coloring or sad and dreary in clothes that work against you. We have all experienced drinking coffee out of a white styrofoam cup versus a richly colored mug. We actually perceive a difference in the taste. Color and design impact us daily.

Color Theory

Color theory begins with the basic color wheel that you studied as a child.

- yellow
- orange

- red
- purple
- blue
- green

Red, yellow, and blue are the primary colors. The secondary colors, a result of mixing primary colors, are orange, green, and purple. Tertiary colors occur when you mix a primary with a secondary color, for example, reddish purple.

The *hue* is the simple name of the color.

The *value* is the lightness or darkness of the color. To tint a color is to lighten it with white. To shade a color is to darken it with black or brown.

The *intensity* of a color is its strength or purity. You can mute a color (reduce its intensity) by mixing it with its complement.

Color schemes and moods are based on using warm or cool colors. The blue-based colors, greens, blues, greenish yellows, and bluish purples, are considered cool colors. (Blue is associated with water.) The red-based colors, oranges, reds, orangish yellows, and reddish purples, are considered warm colors. (Red is associated with fire.) White reflects heat and appears cool, though a yellowish white is warmer than a bluish white. Black absorbs heat and is warm. White and black are considered neutrals in color schemes. Smooth textures appear cool and rough textures, warm.

It makes sense that you would not want to design a very hot room in red, or wear warm colors on a blazing day. This is why red sweaters are very popular in winter and white suits are worn in summer. Colors set temperature perceptions and moods.

Color Schemes

Complementary colors are opposite each other on the color wheel. The red/green colors of Christmas are a complementary color scheme. The colors tend to neutralize each other. In homes, you usually don't use these colors in full strength, but different values of these hues.

Adjacent (analogous) colors are next to each other on the wheel. The blue-green combination is an adjacent color scheme. Adjacent schemes are warmer or cooler than complementary schemes.

Monochromatic schemes employ different values, tones, and textures of one color. A split-complementary scheme employs a color with the two colors adjacent to its opposite complement. Example: Blue with red-orange and yellow-orange.

Triad and tetrad (four colors) schemes can be very effective but are tricky to make work.

Color schemes usually use two to three colors, one major color and one or two accent colors. Light colors appear lighter against a dark background. Dark colors appear darker against a light background.

(See "Imaging Books" in the Bibliography)

FAMILY TRADITIONS: IDEA CHECKLIST

T raditions are the core of a family's identity. Ideas follow to assist you in developing your own distinct traditions.

Inspirations for Traditions

The best traditions are those which are unique to your family. Here are some possible celebration ideas.

You can celebrate famous people with remembering historical events, periods of history, and their countries. For example, you can have an Artists' Renaissance party or cook a German meal on Bach's birthday and listen to his music.

We celebrate Handel's birthday with an English Tea doll party. Tschaikowsky's birthday might be celebrated with a trip to the ballet. Famous artists might be celebrated with a museum trip. One of our favorite celebrations of an author is our "Narnia Kingdom party" on C. S. Lewis' birthday. A Dicken's Christmas is fun at holiday time.

Our celebrations reflect the arts because that is our interest. You may celebrate famous sports figures with game tickets or other seasonal events.

Celebrate a "You Are Special Day" for each member of the family. We chose the birthdate in each month. Six month (½) birthdays are especially fun, complete with half-cakes, half-presents, etc. We include the twenty-fifth (Jesus's birthdate) as Special Kindness Day each month in His honor. Include a child's spiritual birthday, the anniversary of his or her baptism, in the year's festivities as a time of renewal.

Celebrate the anniversaries of other landmark events that you have experienced as a family.

Don't forget special children's days, such as the First Day of School Party, Last Day of School Picnic, Lost Tooth Party. Remember special activity boxs for sick days and graduation/award parties.

"Eve Parties," similar to Christmas Eve, are times of anticipation and preparation which can extend to a week or month! We have a collection of birthday books that we read on Birthday Eve. The "First Day of School Eve Party" can include receiving a new notebook or outfit. Thanksgiving Eve can be a family time of prayer and thankfulness. Each night in November we each write down what we are thankful for and put it in a jar, and we read them all on Thanksgiving Eve.

Combining your unique family celebrations with the general holidays will quickly create a calendar of weekly festivities. Yet you can have a mini-celebration daily. Make one time of the day a priority for spending family time together and do not abandon it when one family member cannot be there. Dinner time is a natural choice but that doesn't work for many families.

On Sunday evening, we write simple activities on cards and put them in a "Treat Jar." Each night we pull one out for the "surprise activity." These are simple activities, such as doing a puzzle, playing a game, or going out for ice cream. We combine it with our dinner time and book/Bible reading at bedtime.

Another favorite dinner time game is pulling questions out of a basket: When were you saddest today? When were you happiest today? What made you laugh today? What made you mad today? It helps us to review the day together, and everyone gets a turn to share.

You can give the days of the week or month special meaning. Maybe Mom makes cookies on Tuesdays. Maybe Friday is popcorn/movie night. Saturday could be an adventure day when you go on outings. We actually call Saturday "Daddy Day" at our house. Though our dad has a very demanding schedule during the week, he always saves Saturdays to plan a surprise for the children. Maybe the first Sunday of the month is "Hospitality Sunday" when you have several friends over for dinner after church.

Incorporate your nightly activities with the season. In December, nightly we light the "1-24 days" candle, open the Advent calendar, sing carols, and pray for friends who have sent us Christmas cards. We also enjoy daily cutting one link off the popular Christmas chain, on it written that day's special activity: a crèche party, tree trimming, Jesus' birthday party, cookie baking, outing to see the *Nutcracker* or *Messiah*.

Integrate your church's traditions with your family festivities. Is there a missions conference? Is there Vacation Bible School in the summer? Are there special holiday services? All these can be wonderful extensions of your family memories.

In addition to the annual party, create a unique way that you celebrate birthdays in your family. It can be breakfast in bed, a special birthday cup, a birthday banner, a treasure hunt for gifts, being Queen or King for a Day, or lunch at a favorite restaurant. Remember that you are creating a family identity that will last a lifetime.

Do not be discouraged if you are always at the homes of extended family on holidays and feel that you cannot develop your own traditions. Simply do them on another day. We usually travel to grandparents at Thanksgiving so we have our Pilgrim Party at home the weekend before.

Keep your traditions recorded in a journal to refer to through the years. This will make for wonderful memories and help plan future celebrations.

Stress the traditions of your ethnic heritage but enjoy the ones of other cultures. For example, we do not have a Chinese heritage, but we have several missionary friends in China. We remember them in special prayer on Chinese New Year.

Plan to celebrate your children's "entrance into adulthood." Will it be when they turn eighteen? graduate from high school? from college? get married? A special gift honoring each year of their life will be a lasting treasure. It may be a collection of letters written yearly. We write letters to each child on her birthday in a journal to be read when she leaves home. You may design a quilt, with a different square made each year. You may collect your family traditions, memories, and recipes in a book. We had a poster entitled "We Were There" for all the guests to sign at each child's first birthday gala celebration. We look forward to reading that poster again at each twenty-first birthday party, by which time many of those toddler scrawls will belong to grown young adults.

The Kindness Project is the most meaningful part of every tradition. It may be supporting a child overseas, visiting a rest home, leaving flowers on a neighbor's doorstep on May Day, gift deliveries, making Valentines, sending a card to a sick friend, or meeting the needs that God shows us.

Every day must be sprinkled with kindness and thoughtfulness but the Kindness Project emphasizes that God gives to us so that we can pass His love on to others. We give our children solid family traditions so that they can share that love and specialness with the world throughout their lives.

Life is not all fun and games! But hard work can be associated with joyous times. Have a backyard picnic lunch on Saturday workdays, a Christmas card addressing party in December, or annual spring cleaning party. Community chores can become family fun.

How To Make a Celebration a Festive Tradition

1. Special Meal: A special meal (FOOD!) is central and should be representative of the theme or country being celebrated. Examples: pumpkin soup and bread on Halloween, Italian food on Columbus Day, corned beef and cabbage on St. Patrick's Day, Chinese food on Chinese New Year, Mexican food on Cinco De Mayo, French food on

Bastille Day, sauerbrauten for Oktoberfest, heart-shaped foods for Valentine's, lamb for Maundy Thursday/Passover. The possibilities are endless.

2. Special Holiday Books: We keep a basket with the "books of the month" on the holiday's themes to be read at bedtime.

3. Music: This can include Easter hymns, Christmas carols, love songs for Valentine's, Irish Harp music for St. Patrick's, or the works of composers. A theme song for each holiday can add a distinctive touch.

4. Decorations: Christmas is not the only time for decorating! We decorate on the first of each month for the respective holidays. Our children especially enjoy re-creating the monthly wreath for the door.

5. Bible Devotions and Prayer: Include a Biblical perspective and prayer. You will be surprised to see in the enclosed calendar how many of our secular traditions have spiritual roots. Valentine's is a time for focusing on verses about love and faithfulness. St. Patrick's Day is a celebration of evangelism. Mistletoe Day is a day of forgiveness.

Calendar

January

  1 New Year's—Time of remembrance and renewal

  6 12th Night—Arrival of the wise men. Children put their shoes out the night before to receive gifts from the wise men.

15 Martin Luther King Day

February

1   Chinese New Year

2   Groundhog Day — Hibernation Day

Candlemas — Jesus is the Light of the World (Christ is the Temple).

14   Valentine's Day — This was originally the anniversary of the death of St. Valentine, a bishop who remained faithful to Christ during Claudius' persecution and was martyred. It is a day of Christian love and faithfulness.

Presidents' birthdays

March

17   St. Patrick's Day — We celebrate St. Patrick, the devoted Christian missionary to Ireland during A.D. 400. He used the shamrock to explain the doctrine of the Trinity.

April

1   April Fools' Day

Palm Sunday

Maundy Thursday — Passover meal — The Last Supper

Good Friday — The Crucifixion

Easter

May

1 May Day — The celebration of spring with May baskets and the May pole.

5 Cinco de Mayo — September 16 is actually Mexico's Independence Day. Cinco de Mayo celebrates a landmark battle against the French army.

Mother's Day

Pentecost — The coming of the Holy Spirit. Celebration of the Trinity.

Memorial Day

June

Father's Day

July

4 Happy Birthday, America

14 Bastille Day — French Independence Day

September

Labor Day Weekend

October

Oktoberfest — German Fall Festival

Columbus Day

Harvest Home — Celebration of home and the fall harvest.

31 Halloween

November

Veteran's Day

Thanksgiving

December

Advent Season — four Sundays

6 St. Nicholas Day — Arrival of St. Nicholas.

12 Poinsettia Day — Celebration of the Mexican flower.

13 St. Lucia Day — Swedish arrival of the Christmas season.

15 Mistletoe Day — Mistletoe is the symbol of forgiving one's enemies.

16 Las Posadas — Latin celebration of Mary and Joseph seeking room at the inn.

24 Christmas Eve

25 Christmas

31 New Year's Eve

APPENDIX D

RESOURCES

Mid-Life Dimensions, Christian Living Resources. P.O. Box 3030, Fullerton, CA 92634. Offers Jim and Sally Conway's *Women in the Mid-Life Crisis.*

American Craft Council, 40 West 53rd Street, New York, NY 10019.

The Personal Touch. Artistic Greetings Stationery Co., P.O. Box 1623, Elmira, NY 14902.

You can study the same design journals that interior designers read: *American Craft, Architectural Digest, Designers West, House Beautiful, House and Garden, Interior Design,* and *Metropolitan Home.*

Homeworking Mothers, a quarterly newsletter. Mother's Home Business Network, Box 423, East Meadow, NY 11554.

Numerous holiday books for children are available from:

Children's Book and Music Center
2500 Santa Monica Boulevard
Santa Monica, CA 90404

BIBLIOGRAPHY

Professional Specialization Books

Bolles, R. N. *What Color Is Your Parachute?* Berkeley, CA: Ten Speed Press, 1988. The definitive guide to seeking career directions, written by a former pastor.

Career Guide to Professional Associations. Garrett Park, MD: Garrett Park Press.

Ekstrom, Ruth B., Abigail M. Harris, and Marlaine E. Lockheed. *How to Get College Credit for What You Have Learned as a Homemaker and Volunteer.* Princeton, NJ: Project HAVE SKILLS, Education Testing Service, 1977. They also publish the *Have Skills Women's Workbook, Have Skills Counselor's Guide,* and *Have Skills Employee's Guide.*

Keisey, D., and M. Bates. *Please Understand Me—Character and Temperament Types.* Del Mar, CA: Prometheus Nemesis Books, 1978. Excellent guide to discovering your temperament.

Pearson, Henry G. *Your Hidden Skills: Clues to Careers and Future Pursuits.* Wayland, MA: Mowry Press, 1981.

Powell, T. *Self-Help Organizations and Professional Practice.* Silver Springs, MD: National Association of Social Workers, 1987.

Rinker, Richard N., and Virginia Eisentrout. *Called to be Gifted and Giving: An Adult Resource for Vocation and Calling.* New York, NY: United Church Press, 1985.

Robbins, Paula I. *Successful Midlife Career Change: Self-Understanding and Strategies for Action.* New York: Amacom.

Wehrheim, Carol, and Ronald S. Cole-Turner. *Vocation and Calling. Introduction/Hearing God's Call/Sharing Gifts: An Intergenerational Study Guide.* New York: United Church Press, 1985.

Organizational Books

Arson, E. and Liden, K. *The Complete Book of Home Management.* Chicago, IL: Moody Press, 1979.

Barnes, E. *More Hours in My Day.* Eugene, OR: Harvest House, 1982.

MacDonald, G. *Ordering Your Private World.* Nashville, TN: Thomas Nelson Publishers, 1985.

Young, Pam and Peggy Jones. *Sidetracked Home Executives.* New York: Warner Books, 1981.

Imaging Books

Ardell, D. *Fourteen Days to a Wellness Lifestyle.* Mill Valley, CA: Whatever Publishing, 1982.

Bailey, C. *Fit or Fat?* Boston, MA: Houghton Mifflin Co., 1977.

Diamonstein, B. *Interior Design.* New York: Rizzoli International, 1982.

Itten, J. *The Art of Color.* New York: Van Nostrand Reinhold, 1961.

Jackson, C. *Color Me Beautiful.* New York: Ballantine Books, 1987.

Molloy, John. *The Woman's Dress for Success Book.* New York: Warner Books, 1977.

Powell, Wm. *The World of Color and How to Use It.* Tustin, CA: Foster Art Services, Inc.

Pile, John. *Interior Design.* New York: Harry Abrams, Inc., 1988.

Business and Marketing Books

Arden, Lynie. *The Work-at-Home Sourcebook.* Boulder, CO: Live Oak Publications, 1987.

Behr, Marion, and Wendy Lazar. *Women Working Home: The Homebased Business Guide and Directory.* Edison, NJ: Women Working Home, Inc., 1983.

Blanchard, K., and S. Johnson. *The One Minute Manager.* New York: William Morrow and Co., 1982.

Comisky, J. *How to Start, Expand and Sell a Business (The Complete Guide for Entrepreneurs).* San Jose, CA: Venture Perspective, 1985.

Davis, R., and G. Smith. *Marketing in Emerging Companies.* Reading, MA: Addison-Wesley Publishers, 1984.

Delany, George and Sandra. *The #1 Home Business Book.* Blue Ridge Summit, PA: Liberty House, 1981.

Drucker, Peter. *Innovation and Entrepreneurship.* New York: Harper and Row, 1985.

Edwards, Paul and Sarah. *Working from Home: Everything You Need to Know about Living and Working Under the Same Roof.* Los Angeles, CA: J. P. Tarcher, Inc., 1985.

Kuriloff and Hemphill. *Starting and Managing a Small Business.* New York: McGraw-Hill, 1983.

Levitt, T. *The Marketing Imagination.* New York: The Free Press, 1983.

McCormack, M. *What They Don't Teach You at Harvard Business School.* New York: Bantam Books, 1984.

Peters, T., and A. Austin. *A Passion for Excellence.* New York: Random House, 1985.

Ries, A., and J. Trout. *Positioning: The Battle for Your Mind.* New York: Warner Books, 1981.

Stress Books

Hart, A. *Adrenalin and Stress.* Waco, TX: Word Books, 1984.

Ogilvie, Lloyd. *Making Stress Work for You.* Waco, TX: Word Books, 1984.

Traditions Books

Begley. *Of Scottish Ways.* New York: Harper and Row Publishers.

Birkey, V., and J. Turnquist. *Building Happy Memories and Family Traditions.* Old Tappan, NJ: Fleming Revell, 1980.

Crager and Grace. *The Whole Christmas Catalogue.* Tucson, AZ: HP Books, 1986.

Delaney. *Of Irish Ways.* New York: Harper and Row.

Depew, A. *The Game Book.* Grand Rapids, MI: Baker Book House, 1960.

Douglas, George William. revised by Helen Douglas Compton. *The American Book of Days.* New York: The H. W. Wilson Co., 1937, 1948.

Dupuy, Trevor Nevitt, ed. *Holidays: Days of Significance for All Americans.* New York: Franklin Watts, 1965.

Franklin, L. *Our Christmas Book.* New York: True Communications, 1981.

Greif, Martin. *The St. Nicholas Book: A Celebration of Christmas Past.* New York: Universe Books, 1976.

Greif, Martin. *The Holiday Book.* New York: Universe Books.

Harbin, E. *Lively Parties for All Occasions.* Grand Rapids, MI: Baker Book House, 1950.

Hooper, ed. *Christmas Around the World.* Wisconsin: Ideals Publications, 1961.

Hunt, G. *Honey for a Child's Heart.* Grand Rapids, MI: Zondervan, 1978.

Krythe, Maymie. *All About American Holidays.* New York: Harper and Row, 1962.

Lorenzen, Lilly. *Of Swedish Ways.* New York: Harper and Row, 1978.

Myers, Robert J. *Celebrations: The Complete Book of American Holidays.* Garden City, New York: Doubleday and Company, Inc., 1972.

Nehmer, N. *A Parent's Guide to Christian Books for Children.* Wheaton, IL: Tyndale House, 1985.

Reilley, T. and M. *Family Nights Throughout the Year.* Indiana: Abbey Press, 1978.

Rickerson, W., *Family Fun and Togetherness*. Wheaton, IL: Victor Books, 1979.

Rio, Rydberg, and Yaconelli. *Fun 'N Games*. Grand Rapids, MI: Zondervan. 1977.

Rippley, Lavern. *Of German Ways*. New York: Harper and Row, 1979.

Robinson, H. W., ed. *Families Are Fun*. Christian Medical Society, 1977.

Rockwell, N. *Norman Rockwell's Christmas Book*. New York: Abrams, 1977.

Royds. *The Christmas Book*. New York: G. P. Putnam, 1985.

Walker, G., ed. *The Celebration Book*. Glendale, CA: Regal Books, 1977.

ABOUT THE AUTHOR

M ary Ann Froehlich holds a doctorate in music education/music therapy from the University of Southern California, a M.A. degree in Theology (pastoral care) from Fuller Theological Seminary, and M.A. and B.M. degrees in piano and harp performance and music therapy.

She is also a certified Child Life Specialist and has published her dissertation research on the use of music therapy with chronically and terminally ill children.

A Suzuki music educator and Registered Music Therapist-Board Certified, Mary Ann has worked in hospitals, schools, churches, and private practice. She is a frequent contributor to professional journals. Her piano/harp arrangements are published with FC Publishing Company.

Dr. Froehlich lives in Benicia, California with her husband, John, and their three children; Janelle, Natalie, and Cameron.

The typeface for the text of this book is *Times Roman*. In 1930, typographer Stanley Morison joined the staff of *The Times* (London) to supervise design of a typeface for the reformatting of this renowned English daily. Morison had overseen type-library reforms at Cambridge University Press in 1925, but this new task would prove a formidable challenge despite a decade of experience in paleography, calligraphy, and typography. *Times New Roman* was credited as coming from Morison's original pencil renderings in the first years of the 1930s, but the typeface went through numerous changes under the scrutiny of a critical committee of dissatisfied *Times* staffers and editors. The resulting typeface, *Times Roman*, has been called the most used, most successful typeface of this century. The design is of enduring value to English and American printers and publishers, who choose the typeface for its readability and economy when run on today's high-speed presses.

Substantive Editing:
Michael S. Hyatt

Copy Editing:
Susan Kirby

Cover Design:
Kent Puckett Associates, Atlanta, Georgia

Page Composition:
Xerox Ventura Publisher
Printware 720 IQ Laser Printer

Printing and Binding:
Maple-Vail Book Manufacturing Group,
York, Pennsylvania

Cover Printing:
Strine Printing Company, Inc.
York, Pennsylvania